THE CHANGING COMPOSITION OF THE
WORKFORCE
Implications for Future Research and Its Application

THE CHANGING COMPOSITION OF THE
WORKFORCE

Implications for Future Research and Its Application

Edited by
Albert S. Glickman

Old Dominion University
Norfolk, Virginia

PLENUM PRESS · NEW YORK AND LONDON

Library of Congress Cataloging in Publication Data

Main entry under title:

The Changing composition of the workforce.

"Proceedings of the Second Annual Scientist—Practitioner Conference in Industrial/Organizational Psychology, held April 23–24, 1981, at Old Dominion University, Norfolk, Virginia"—Verso t.p.
  Bibliography: p.
  Includes index.
  1. Labor supply—United States—Forecasting—Congresses. 2. Aged—Employment—United States—Forecasting—Congresses. 3. Youth—Employment—United States—Forecasting—Congresses. 4. College graduates—Employment—United States—Forecasting—Congresses. 5. Employment of men—United States—Forecasting—Congresses. 6. Women—Employment—United States—Forecasting—Congresses. 7. Industrial relations—United States—Forecasting—Congresses. I. Glickman, Albert S. II. Scientist—Practitioner Conference in Industrial/Organizational Psychology (2nd: 1981: Old Dominion University)
HD5724.C48   331.11'4'0973   82-615
ISBN 0-306-40995-X   AACR2

Proceedings of The Second Annual Scientist – Practitioner Conference
in Industrial/Organizational Psychology, held April 23 – 24, 1981,
at Old Dominion University, Norfolk, Virginia

©1982 Plenum Press, New York
A Division of Plenum Publishing Corporation
233 Spring Street, New York, N.Y. 10013

Printed in the United States of America

PREFACE

The Annual Scientist-Practitioner Conferences in Industrial-Organizational Psychology were conceived by the Department of Psychology at Old Dominion University as a means to foster exchange of information, points of view, and insights among those who are engaged in research in the behavioral and social sciences, and those who, in various business, industrial, managerial, organizational, and educational roles, are actively engaged in work affording opportunities to apply the findings and concepts generated by scientific study (many people do both). Our vested interest and our hope is that the stimulus provided by these exchanges will help us and our professional cohorts in psychology and other disciplines to advance the cutting edge of theory and application in problem areas of present and prospective importance. The first of these conferences took place in 1980, and had as its theme, "Performance Appraisal." The papers here constitute the substantive contributions to the second conference which addressed issues pertinent to "The Changing Composition of the Workforce."

It should be noted that although industrial-organizational psychologists continue to claim parentage, this meeting can lay claim to an interdisciplinary lineage, validated by the presence on its panels and among the other invited participants of economists, labor officials, educators, personnel administrators, gerontologists, sociologists, business managers, and military officers, as well as others of unknown origins.

Four half-day panel presentations followed by open discussion considered issues with regard to changes in age composition and in gender composition, and to implications for management and labor and for higher education. No prescriptions were given to the scientist and practitioner panelists in each area other than that they be provocative and seek to highlight "implications for future research and its application." The vitality of discussion that was generated in each instance demonstrated the success with which they responded to that charge.

    For their contributions, profound gratitude is due to the panelists; particularly because they had the distinction of being among the first to bear the sacrifice imposed by economies enforced by the incoming federal administration. Because expected funding was "frozen", no tangible reward for their efforts could be provided. To Raymond H. Kirby, Chair, Department of Psychology, Old Dominion University, go thanks for extracting from departmental funds the operational and panelist travel expenses that made it possible to put our plans for this Conference into effect.

    The spirited and constructive inputs to discussion that came from the others in attendance -- to some degree assimilated in the final publication drafts here -- added substantially to the intellectual and social ambience of the meeting. The conduct of the Conference was also facilitated by the volunteer efforts of students in the ODU doctoral program in Industrial-Organizational Psychology and the administrative assistance of Nancy K. Eberhardt, Research Specialist. The burdens of the editor were eased by Elizabeth S. Henry, Associate Professor of Psychology, who initiated liaison with the publisher; by Sarah B. Sands, Secretary, Center for Applied Psychological Studies, who carried a large part of the responsibility for preparation in advance of the Conference and for the preparation of the manuscript of these proceedings, assisted by Karen Lound and Renee Lied; and Patricia M. Vann, Associate Editor, our principal contact at Plenum Publishing Corporation. To all of these, I express my great appreciation.

                                                        Albert S. Glickman

CONTENTS

INTRODUCTION

CHARTING A COURSE

Albert S. Glickman

Old Dominion University

Norfolk, VA

Conference Genesis, Themes and Objectives

What changes can we expect in the years ahead that will have major effects upon the world of work and our life styles? Already in place as a crucial determinant is the changing mix of our population. Quite obviously, this condition creates a need to put research in applied psychology and management science in a proactive posture; that is, to try to anticipate the problems that lie ahead and the research that should be started now to meet them, as Robert Miller (1977) has put it, "so that storm centers can be anticipated early enough to enable their dissipation" (p. 420). Related to this is the persistent charge that academia, and the research enterprise that it sponsors, provide the tools and create a mind set better suited to meet conditions faced by the last generation than the next generation. So it is that, just as the nation has come to the realization that it confronts a future in which it must draw upon a different mix of energy resources, it must also now take into account that significant changes are taking place in the mix of its human resources.

Some things we can see taking place now. These are linked to changes we can predict with considerable certainty. Although the delphic forecasts of the futurists provide a variety of scenarios, a reasonable degree of consensus can be established. But how to cope with future changes represents a lot of uncertainty. There lies opportunity for worthwhile research.

As a first step toward a program of behavioral and social science research centering on problems expected to accompany changes

in the adult population mix, the Center for Applied Psychological
Studies of the Old Dominion University conducted an invitational
conference in April of 1981. The proceedings of that conference
brought forth the contributions which are the chapters of this book.
The generation of these articles and the publication of this book
have been guided by three programmatic purposes: (1) to assess the
state of our knowledge and sophistication with regard to prominent
problems and issues that need to be better defined and confronted,
that will stem from foreseeable changes in the composition of the
work force and population at large and in the nature of work and
life style in the years ahead; (2) to elevate the state of readiness
of the relevant communities of scientists, professional practitioners, and business, labor and government leaders to address such
problems and issues in an efficient and timely fashion; and (3) to
help in formulating a research prospectus that could provide a prod
and guide to shaping the objectives, priorities and design of
projects to be undertaken during the next several years.

     The sizeable literature that has been accumulating depicting
future scenarios for the world of work, non-work and life styles in
a post-industrial society has raised many important questions of
policy and practice. However, for the most part, these questions
have not been converted into research propositions. We propose to
take a step in that direction by focusing this effort upon research
that can be initiated at this time to enhance our ability to anticipate and to cope with such questions, particularly as they are
affected by the prospective changes in the composition of the population, of the nature and organization of work, and of interrelated
contextual factors.

Background, Issues and Focus of Investigation

     When undertaking an examination of the implications for future
research that derive from the changing composition of the work
force, a wide panorama opens up. Practical constraints therefore
require that in the beginning our efforts be governed by rationally
determined priorities and limits of scope. Thus, at this stage of
the research program development, we get underway from a point of
departure that first considers the largest, recent and prospective
components of population shift in the workforce, the demographic
macrowaves represented by age and gender. Of course, within this
framework, exploration cannot proceed without including in our
developing picture of the future other population groups, indivi-
dually and in combination, as defined by race and origin, physical
or mental handicaps, occupation, income, marital status, geographic
location, et al. Two charts, drawn from a recent presentation by
the Director of the Census (Barabba, 1980), give graphic impact to
data on age and gender population trends.

To represent the nature of the matters to be considered, we need not be exhaustive at this point. It is sufficient to look at a few sample situations.

We know that the average age of the population and work force will be increasing, as reflected in Figure 1. The birthrate has been decreasing; longevity has been increasing. The age of entry into matrimony and employment has gone up while the age of retirement has trended downward along with the number of days at work in the period between. Among the questions that arise: What will be the eventual outcome of legislation that takes the lid off mandatory retirement age? Will it stem the decline in average age of retirement? How will career motivation and job motivation be affected? Does the share and focus of research need to shift to correspond with the increased proportion of life spent off-the-job?

We know that the post-war baby boom (the unshaded bars in Figure 1) is pushing a bulge through the population distribution that now is approaching the prime years of worklife, creating unprecedented competition for positions and promotion across the full spectrum of the economy, whether the condition be depression or prosperity. Perhaps equal employment opportunity will take on new meanings as "young" people in their 30's and 40's find their upward mobility blocked by increased proportions of the population in their 50's and 60's. Already we are struggling to assimilate in our economic, political and social value systems the consequences of the transformation of the age-sex distribution from the historic pyramid to the atypical rectangle that our chart displays.

We also know that in the last generation the economy has experienced a massive infusion of working women, as Figure 2 shows. At last count about 60% of working age women were actually employed and about half of these had family responsibilities. Against the social norms of previous generations, they are doing some mighty "odd" jobs.

So we have women climbing poles for the telephone companies, and having more than their share of accidents. Which has occasioned considerable research to fit the job to females through research on equipment design and physical training.

At the other end we have a steadily mounting representation of women in managerial ranks accompanied by the personal and organizational adjustments accompanying this transitional state. For example, in a decade the number of female MBA's has risen from 100 to 15,000 per year. It is also worth making note of the recent Census report that at age 35 and above, the number of female college graduates again enrolled is twice that of men.

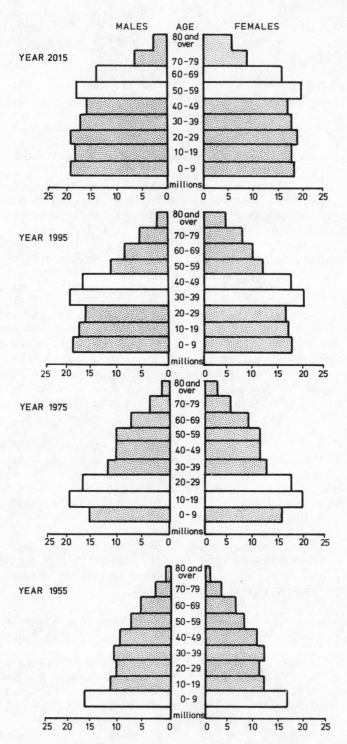

Figure 1. U.S. Population by Age and Sex: 1955–2015. (Source:
U.S. Bureau of the Census.)

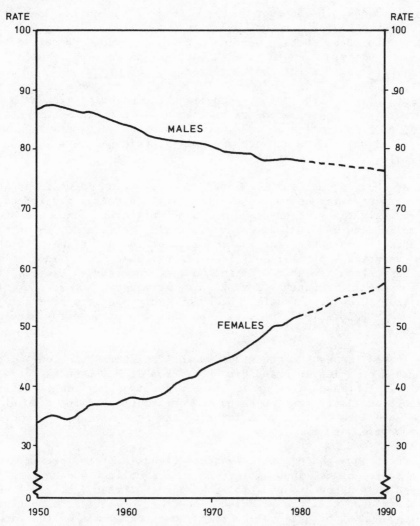

Figure 2. Labor Force Participation Rates for Persons by Sex:
          1950 to 1990. (Source: U.S. Bureau of the Census.)

    On another tack, we observe that until now child care has been
thought of largely in the context of welfare benefits for poor
people. We might ask how long it will be before every sizeable work
site will include a nursery, and what this will mean for psychologists, teachers, social workers, physicians, health scientists, and
labor leaders and managers of various persuasions.

    A pattern of increased flexibility of work and non-work sched-
ules is emerging reinforced by legislation. This is generally seen

as a "good thing." However, new problems of personal adjustment,
social-psychological and organizational dynamics, and logistics,
come to the fore. Not to mention a revival of concern relevant to
classic studies of length of work periods and fatigue, productivity,
safety, span of control, and so forth.

Interacting with the foregoing is the continuing growth in computerization, communication technology and other accompaniments of
the "post-industrial society" that will, within a generation, markedly alter the nature of work and work sites, and the style and
quality of life in general.

Pay check deductions regularly call attention to what happens as
the ratio of retirees to workers goes up. Industry, government, and
increasingly the younger worker in particular, are concerned with
the ballooning of absolute costs of funding retirement, as well as
the effect upon retirement and concepts of incentive and motivation.
Thus, we note that retirement benefits are assuming an increasingly
prominent place in labor negotiations, as recently illustrated in
the automobile industry. For example, at General Motors there is
one person drawing a pension check for every 3.3 persons drawing a
paycheck. Before 1999 there will be only two at work for each on
pension.

Kindred issues confront the domain of higher education and the
resources of scientists and discovery that it has been expected to
provide. Increased age and tenure of faculty alongside of declining
student enrollment creates a severe constriction of the flow of "new
blood" and intellectual vitality into the academic and the social
and economic system.

One wonders whether the times and trends call for reexamination
and some redesign. Thus, forecasts of the college and university
student body appear to be still conditioned almost exclusively by
the assumption that the principal "customer" pool is the population
not long out of high school. Given the changing mix of the population, is there need for a fresh needs assessment from a vantage
point that gives consideration to other potential clientele, different recruiting strategies, and other curricular designs than those
now employed? Might we be led to revised assumptions as undergirds
of policy, which might then lead to revised goals based upon expectations of continuing increase in the student body; if curricula
were designed specifically for well defined segments of more mature
men and women; if many of these potential clients were not "turned
off" by the perception that to reenter the work force or take a new
occupational direction, or to revise or redirect a career, one must
regress to post-adolescence and surrender status and stimulus acquired through experience and achievement?

To keep abreast of the increasing rate of change might we find it useful to devise social indicators, to go along with periodic reports of cost of living, consumer intentions, and the like, that could give us timely anticipation of changes in patterns of values, needs and beliefs affecting work and free-time activities, to re-place the wistful, time-lagged, eternally ambiguous, retrospective observation that time and old values have changed? Might these kinds of social indicators serve a need for consistent criterion measures to evaluate impact of interventions by government, through education, and in business and industry? Could they increase under-standing of the forces at work in increasing or decreasing labor force participation of women and men from different segments of the population and at different points in their life history?

This list of these examples and the questions they arouse could be extended almost endlessly. We have chosen only a few that have been salient in our experience and research. Again, we are obliged to set limits for our first stage efforts. So we have chosen to focus attention initially upon implications for and applications of future research in two domains: (1) Labor and management of the '90's, and (2) Higher education for the '90's. These choices are governed by the immediate social and economic significance of the forthcoming changes to population and workforce in these sectors and by the professional and scientific experience and competencies we can bring to bear upon the study of related impacts, innovations and implications. In the first instance, it is self-evident that man-agement and labor leadership are most directly involved in shaping the plans, policies, and procedures to deal constructively with the revised organizational style, structure and context that these radi-cal alterations in the makeup of the workforce will impose, and the continuing need to revive and sustain productivity growth in an era that is also marked by an unprecedented metamorphosis in technology.

Most of the writers who speak of the changes that lie ahead have dealt with the composition of the workforce at the level of macro-trend projections, from which they spin off a host of speculations (like the sampling we have offered above). Their general tenor has been: Look out; the fallout of problems will be many and the conse-quences often severe. One of the most recent collections, assembled by Kerr and Rosow (1979), can serve as an example. Because, the focus is upon general trends, the authors tend correspondingly to treat the mechanisms of adjustment largely at the general policy level. However, the time has come to move from the global reaches of demographics and economics to where the shoes will pinch in op-erational settings; in specific business, industrial, educational and governmental organizations; where the people are who will first and most directly have to come to grips with problems we have been talking about. In the usual pattern, the accumulation of their hurts, where they live and work, will create the impetus for more encompassing policy formulation. Consequently, we eventually expect

to center our sphere of research upon relatively self-contained
organizational units as they confront and try to cope with problems
posed by the substantial workforce changes. Some of these problem
symptoms are already being manifested. Furthermore, it is within
such boundaries that it is feasible to carry out systematic observations, track change processes, and assess results of interventions,
under various conditions imposed by endogenous and exogenous
factors.

As for higher education, the future is now. It is the colleges
and universities who have a critical role in creating an awareness
in their students of critical issues of the kind we have articulated
that will soon confront them as citizens and as managers and professionals, and in contributing the educational wherewithal to cope
with them. That they also bear a large responsibility for making
the necessary research contributions goes without saying. Nor can
it be ignored that the institutions of higher education are even now
being sharply impacted by these population shifts that do not fit
comfortably with their traditional modus vivendi.

A Research Prospectus

The authors represented in this book go a long way toward
defining the critical issues, knowledge and methodological gaps, and
needs for theory and research in its areas of consideration. It is
to be hoped that the stimulus which they provide will give impetus
to research undertaking to meet the needs anticipated. While we do
not presume to anticipate the creative outcomes of the readers of
these articles, it may be helpful to engage in some preliminary
speculation. So, without aspiring to be comprehensive, we will give
a few examples (just three) of how and where research in this area
might be applied.

What do people know and expect. One direction that research
might follow early on could be to assemble some basic data on what
various segments of the population know about the changing work
force and what they anticipate may be the consequences and the
personal, social and organizational adjustments that will be called
for. One suspects that gaps exist between the forecasts professionals have published and the level of awareness of men and women
in factories, offices, government agencies, unions and universities
at various hierarchical levels. The magnitude of such differences
translates as lag in readiness to accept initiatives intended to
facilitate accommodation to changing conditions. Until the "facts"
become tangible and comprehensible for substantial numbers of
people, preferably before they are directly impacted and personally
affected, the best laid plans will be impeded. Our experience with
energy and environmental programs and policies stand as illustrative
analogs. We have already pointed to the sharp awareness of the

results of an aging population induced by social security cost
assessments. Are those who are now in their first generation as
working people as explicitly cognizant of what it may mean to be a
member of the baby boom cohort? How many executives and educators
are taking anticipatory actions? How many are being pushed by the
currents of change only when they are caught up in the flow? Some
organizations are becoming sensitive to these questions.

Longitudinal study. Pursuing the flow metaphor, suggests the
possibility of longitudinal study in businesses, industrial organizations, public agencies, educational institutions, that are already
being or soon will be substantially impacted by population changes,
to see how they have responded and to learn what distinguishes the
successful from the ineffective adaptor organization units. This
would serve to identify the full range of variables and processes to
be identified that, interacting with population changes, affect
adjustments and outcomes of interest (e.g., socio-technological
changes, industrial relations policies and practices, worker participation, equal employment opportunity, work schedules, free time
activities), and permit one to move toward construction of conceptual models.

Changing values, needs and motives. Kanter and Stein (1980), in
a recent paper addressing value changes as related to labor force
trends, raise questions about management problems that may be accompaniments, given a scenario of slower-growth economy, work force
reductions and higher expectations. Some extracts (p. 74) can serve
to suggest experimental interventions, evaluations and research that
could be undertaken.

"How can the desires of increasing numbers of people (women,
minorities, those who go to school longer) for 'meaningful
work' that produces 'career growth' be accommodated within a
... labor market with structural limitations on the proportions
that can experience upward mobility?"

"How can openings be created for younger, educated workers to
exercise their skills when older employees fail to step aside
and have the legal right (civil service, tenure, etc.) to retain their jobs?"

"How can the tension between the higher expectations of the
larger population of longer-educated young 'baby boom' workers
and their limited experience be resolved?"

"If ... jobs are decreasingly less satisfying ... and leisure
and family lives are increasingly more important, is the
'solution' to new values and a productivity crisis to emphasize
time off rather than for personal improvement and development?"

Such dilemmas call for new styles of learning, new designs for jobs and organizations, new ways to use and reward people and to expand the opportunity and power available on jobs at all levels—actions that may very well require a view of management and of management's and labor's roles, and of education and the university's role, that are much different than they are today.

References

Barabba, Vincent P. The economic and demographic impact of the baby boom generation—past, present, and future. Address to the National Economist Club, Washington, D.C., June 10, 1980.

Kanter, Rosabeth M., & Stein, Barry A. Value change and the public work force: labor force trends, the salience of opportunity and power and implications for public sector management. In The changing character of the public work force (Proceedings of the Second Public Management Research Conference). Washington, D.C.: U.S. Office of Personnel Management, 1980.

Kerr, Clark, & Rosow, Jerome M. (Eds.). Work in America: The decade ahead. New York: Van Nostrand Reinhold, 1979.

Miller, Robert M. Human aspects of systems. In B. von Haller Gilmer and Edward L. Deci, Industrial and organizational psychology (4th ed.). New York: McGraw-Hill, 1977.

PART I

THE 1990 AGE MIX

WHEN IS OLD?

Harold L. Sheppard

National Council on the Aging

Washington, D.C.

1 want to talk today about some major themes concerning age and
work, and try to wire in some policy dimensions.

In connection with the topic of this panel, I would like to recommend the April 20 issue of Business Week magazine. It has an excellent article on Japan's aging workforce. The article highlights
many of the problems we are undergoing, but in Japan, they are undergoing it in a much more rapid fashion than we are. I've been keeping
track of that country's work and aging issues and retirement issues
for some years. They fixed the retirement age, or pensionable age,
at age 55 around World War II because the average death age was 55.
Always remember that somewhere along the line, a society's retirement
age does have or did have a reality base.

It does not mean we keep up with the reality base -- Japan is an
example. Their average death age now is 75 and until recently, in
fact, in most of Japan still, the pattern of pensionable age has been
55, based on the pre-World War II mortality data. That has been
creating fantastic problems for Japan. That is not what the Business
Week article is about; it is about the other side of the coin as seen
by managers: what do you do with an aging workforce? -- as seen by
younger workers who feel blocked by those older workers, for example.
Underlying a lot of these types of discussions is what we in the
field of gerontology call ageism. It is analogous to, if not identical with, sexism or racism. I want you to keep that in mind. I will
only give one example of how it plays a role. It seems to me that we
take it culturally for granted that it is the younger worker who
should be preferred in the allocation of jobs over the older worker.
This is a sort of Pavlovian response on the part of a lot of people
saying we have got to make room for the younger workers. That is

15

settled and people go on to the next discussion, without anybody ever
saying: "Why can't there be such a thing as a equitable distribution
of the jobs?" Of course, underlying a lot of the ageism is the
stereotype that increasing age invariably means decreasing work capacity. That is just not true for a great many occupations and in a
great many industries.

Let me get back to my written comments. I want to talk about
something I've been focusing on in the last several months and that
is the point that we are undergoing in our society what I call a redefinition of "when is old." I want to discuss some of the implications of that.

Secondly, I want to call attention to what we call the heterogeneity of the aged population. It is time we stopped using the sloppy
category of "sixty-five plus." that category contains too many age
groups within itself, and the age composition of that category is
undergoing great changes. A lot of people are making policy decisions looking at government tables that simply present or use the
sloppy category of "sixty-five plus."

The other heterogeneity dimension has to do with the sex distribution of that older population -- it is heavily female. This fact
has a lot of work and retirement income implications.

We are undergoing now what I would call a socio-cultural redefinition of when is old. No longer can the age of 65 be virtually universally accepted as the beginning of aging or the time when we join
the category of aged Americans. I believe that the 1978 amendments
to the 1967 Age Discrimination in Employment Act, raising the allow-
able compulsory retirement age to 70, is a concrete example of what
is taking place. Those amendments are a concrete, formal milestone
or reflection of this redefinition process. I am not saying that the
legislators looked at it the way I am looking at it, but I am trying
to step back, in this case, as a cultural analyst to see what is
going on.

In 1974, the National Council on the Aging conducted a very
large, national sample survey, of people 18 to 64 and of the 65-plus
population, to get at some of the myths and realities of aging in
America; how the general public felt about the aged and about aging;
and how the 65-plus population felt about the same things. It was
done through Louis Harris Associates. We are now about to do it
again, in 1981, and that is my major responsibility for the next
several months at the National Council on the Aging. As far as the
specific topic today is concerned, that study revealed that roughly
half of the general public felt that nonchronological factors should
be considered in response to the question that asked, "When does the
typical man or typical or average man or average woman start to

become old?" They gave predominantly non-chronological answers.
Among those who did give a chronological age answer, the average age
was about 62.5 years. We are going to ask this question again, to
determine whether or not the proportion has changed.

My belief is that over the past seven years, the proportion of
Americans giving a non-chronological answer has increased, and/or
that the average chronological age has increased. In the world of
work, this image or perception as to "when is old" is important. For
example, we also have asked respondents their agreement or disagree-
ment with the statement that: "Older people should retire when they
can to give younger people more of a chance on the job."

Any analysis of the responses to this question, it seems to me,
should first take into account the image that respondents have when
the term "older people" is evoked. It must influence the response of
the individual being asked the question.

If a person believes that "older" refers to workers 50 and older,
that is quite different from an image of "older" meaning 60 or 65 and
older. And if I am correct in the belief that the social definition
of "when is old" is changing, then we should expect some degree of
corresponding change in the 1981 survey responses to this critical
question from those in the earlier 1974 survey.

Incidentally, in a 1977 study of approximately 900 employed persons 40-69 years old in two labor market areas, we found that age was
not a factor in their responses to that same question. The critical
factors were: (1) the unemployment experience in recent years of the
individual; and (2) whether or not the individual -- with or without
any unemployment experience -- was in a high or low unemployment
area. The fact that age was not found to be related may, of course,
be due to the fact that our sample consisted of workers 40 and older.
We will be in a better position, with the data from the national survey of 1981, to determine whether workers 18 to 40 years old will respond to the same question partly as a function of their being
younger.

In 1977, persons with some unemployment experience and/or resid-
ing in a high jobless area -- regardless of age -- were the most
likely to agree that older persons should retire to make room for
younger workers. Thus, the problems of work and aging, and the challenge to management of an aging workforce, cannot be separated from
the broader issues of employment policy in this country. The pressures on older workers to retire are not constant. They vary according to economic conditions. Jobless levels lead in one direction and
levels of inflation can lead in an opposite direction, i.e., older
workers may tend to postpone complete retirement when high inflation
rates persist.

One piece of suggestive evidence that inflation may be slowing down retirement is derived from the rate of change in the three averages of retired worker awards under Social Security. While the 1972-74 average of such awards was 9.1 percent greater than the average for the previous three years, the 1975-77 average was only 4.9 percent greater than the 1972-74 average; and the average number of awards for the past three years (1978, 1979, and 1980) -- when high inflation rates persisted -- was only 2.7 percent higher.

On the broader policy level, the issue of encouraging retirement as a way of solving younger workers' job problems must be balanced against the second issue of the degree to which the working population is willing to pay for the increased costs of supporting an older non-working population -- especially if a resolution of the first issue results in an even greater population of retirees. Rarely, if ever, do survey researchers pose a question that juxtaposes both of these isues for survey respondents.

Finally, we must begin to tackle the topic of management adaptations to an older workforce in many, if not most or all, industries. A smaller youth labor force entry group is the underlying basis for this expectation. As only one example, there is the issue of skill obsolescence, plateauing, or "burn-out."

It seems to me that we can no longer accept the view that such phenomena are the result of inexorable processes exclusively due to so-called natural psycho-physiological "aging." Such a view is a comforting one to managers, especially career development personnel. Only recently has there been some recognition that management itself is a factor in this phenomenon.

Middle-aged employees typically are ignored in career development programs. Skill-updating opportunities too frequently are not made available to them. In certain skills, there are severe shortages, some of which could be remedied through reaching out to workers older than those typically recruited for skilled-worker training, including apprenticeship programs.

Redeployment and "second-career" programs also should be considered. And for the older groups of workers, new work-time arrangements, including relatively permanent part-time positions, need to be further explored, as part of what employers might be doing in programs designed to cope with an aging workforce.

THE AGE MIX OF THE LABOR FORCE IN 1990:

IMPLICATIONS FOR LABOR MARKET RESEARCH

Paul J. Andrisani and Thomas N. Daymont

Temple University

Philadelphia, PA

The Age Mix of the Labor Force in 1990

Assessing future changes in labor force composition is a prerequisite to understanding the problems and opportunities that such changes produce. A natural starting point for assessing these future changes is the labor force projections that are provided by the Bureau of Labor Statistics approximately every two years. The projected age distributions for 1990 and 1995 from the most recent projections have been reproduced in Table 1 along with the actual distributions for 1970 and 1979 (Fullerton, 1980)[1]. In Table 2 actual and projected labor force participation rates for these same years and age groups are also reproduced. These projections suggest that the age distribution of the labor force will change significantly over the next decade and that the nature of these changes will differ from the changes that took place during the 1970s.

Due primarily to the coming of age of the baby boom cohort, and secondarily to continued increases in labor force participation rates among young women and the continued decline in labor force participation rates among older men (Table 2), the number of 20-34 year olds as a proportion of the total labor force grew dramatically during the 1970s. This represents a continuation of a significant trend that began in the 1960s. In sharp contrast, the number of 16 to 24 year old youths as a percentage of the labor force will

---

[1]These distributions are based on the "middle growth" projections. The projected age distributions are not very sensitive to the different growth assumptions used by Fullerton.

Table 1.   Age Distribution of Labor Force, Actual and Projected, for
           1970, 1979, 1990, and 1995 and Changes in the Age
           Distribution by Sex

Age	Actual		Projected		Actual change	Projected change
	1970	1979	1990	1995	1970-1979	1979-1980

A. Men

Age	1970	1979	1990	1995	1970-1979	1979-1980
Total	61.9	57.8	53.8	53.0	-4.1	-4.0
16-24	11.7	12.8	9.2	8.3	1.1	-3.6
16-19	4.8	4.8	3.4	3.2	.0	-1.4
20-24	6.9	8.0	5.7	5.0	1.1	-2.3
25-54	38.9	36.1	37.7	38.2	-2.8	1.6
25-34	13.7	15.3	15.0	13.3	1.6	-0.3
35-44	12.6	11.0	13.6	14.3	-1.6	2.6
45-54	12.6	9.7	9.0	10.5	-2.9	-0.7
55+	11.2	8.8	6.9	6.4	-2.4	-1.9
55-64	8.6	6.9	5.4	5.0	-1.7	-1.5
65+	2.6	1.9	1.4	1.3	-0.7	-0.5

B. Women

Age	1970	1979	1990	1995	1970-1979	1979-1980
Total	38.1	42.1	46.1	46.9	4.0	4.0
16-24	9.8	11.1	9.2	8.7	1.3	-1.9
16-19	3.9	4.3	3.4	3.3	0.4	-0.9
20-24	5.9	6.8	5.8	5.4	0.9	-1.0
25-54	22.0	25.4	32.2	33.7	3.4	6.8
25-34	7.1	10.8	13.5	12.5	3.7	2.7
35-44	7.1	7.9	11.9	13.0	0.8	4.0
45-54	7.8	6.6	6.7	8.1	-1.2	0.1
55+	6.3	5.5	4.6	4.4	-0.8	-0.9
55-64	5.0	4.4	3.6	3.5	-0.6	-0.8
65+	1.3	1.1	1.0	0.9	-0.2	-0.1
Total labor force size (in thousands)	82,715	102,908	122,375	127,542		

Sources: Tables 5 and 6 (Middle growth projection) in Fullerton, (1980); Table 5 in Flaim, and
          Fullerton, (1978).

decrease rather dramatically over the next 10 years, while the
percentage of 35 to 44 year old workers will surge.

Despite an assumption of sustained high levels of labor force
participation among young men (Table 2), the number of men between
the ages 16 and 24 as a percentage of the total labor force is expected to drop from 12.8 to 9.1 percent between 1979 and 1990 and to
8.3 percent by 1995 (Table 1). Further, after assuming a continued
strong growth in participation rates among 16-24 year old young
women, from 63 percent to 74 percent between 1979 and 1990 and to

Table 2.   Labor Force Participation Rates, Actual and Projected for
           1970, 1979, 1990, and 1995 by Sex and Age

	Actual		Projected	
Age	1970	1979	1990	1995

A. Men

	1970	1979	1990	1995
Total	79.7	77.9	77.2	76.8
16-24	69.4	77.9	76.8	76.1
16-19	56.1	61.7	64.7	64.7
20-24	83.3	86.6	86.4	85.7
24-54	95.8	94.4	93.7	93.4
25-34	96.0	95.4	94.3	94.0
35-44	96.5	95.8	95.2	95.1
45-54	93.9	91.4	90.8	90.6
55+	55.7	44.2	39.6	37.6
55-64	83.0	73.0	67.5	66.5
65+	26.8	20.0	15.8	14.3

B. Women

	1970	1979	1990	1995
Total	43.3	51.0	59.6	61.2
16-24	41.3	62.6	73.9	77.0
16-19	44.0	54.5	63.9	66.3
20-24	57.7	69.1	81.4	85.3
25-54	50.1	62.2	75.9	78.0
25-34	45.0	63.8	80.7	83.7
35-44	51.0	63.6	78.6	81.7
45-54	54.4	58.4	64.3	66.2
55+	25.3	23.2	20.7	20.2
55-64	43.0	41.9	41.7	42.8
65+	9.7	8.3	7.3	6.8

Sources: Table 3 in Flaim, and Fullerton, (1978); Table 4 (Middle
           growth projection) in Fullerton, (1980).

parity with young men by 1995 at 77 percent (Table 2), their representation as a proportion of the labor force is expected to decrease
from 11.1 to 9.2 percent over the next decade and to only 8.7 percent by 1995 (Table 1).

The effect of the aging of the baby boom cohort on the age distribution of the labor force also shows up clearly in the changing
proportions of 35-44 year old workers, particularly females. During
the 1970s, the older members of the baby boom cohort entered the 25-
34 year old age group, and coupled with the considerable rise in
labor force participation rates among women in this age group (from
45 to 64 percent), their representation in the work force increased
substantially. Over the next decade they will be replaced in this
age group by the second half of the baby boom cohort, and there will
be a slight decline in the representation of young men and a more
modest increase in the representation of 25 to 34 year old young
women in the labor force. Moreover, the increase among women is due
solely to the fact that labor force participation rates are expected
to continue rising for them from 64 to 81 percent by 1990 (Table 2).
Meanwhile, the older baby boomers--and particularly females--will
swell the ranks of the 35 to 44 year old age group, increasing its
size dramatically and perhaps the importance of such age related
problems as mid-life crises, reconciling dual careers, and age discrimination in employment.

Finally, although much has been written recently about the graying of America, it will not be until after the turn of the century
that the baby boom cohort will be old enough to increase the proportion of older workers. Indeed, these projections suggest that the
proportion of older workers (i.e., 55 and over) in the labor force
will actually decrease over the next 10 to 15 years (Table 1), as
labor force participation rates among older workers are expected to
continue their decline (Table 2). One way to summarize the changing
age pattern of the work force is to note that while the median age
of workers was 40 years in 1960 and dropped to 35 years in 1979, it
is expected to increase to 37.5 years by 1995 (Fullerton, 1980).

Labor Force Projections: Methods and Problems

Before these projections can be used with confidence to develop
agendas for research policy, their accuracy needs to be evaluated.
On this score the BLS projections have been subjected to considerable criticism. Most often, they have been criticized for consistently underestimating the number of female and student participants, as well as the total size of the labor force (e.g., Sum,
1977; Smith, 1977; Wachter, 1977). In addition, these projections
have overestimated the number of older workers relative to younger
workers (Freeman, 1979). That is, they have consistently underesti-
mated the increasing labor force participation rates of youths and
females and the declining labor force participation rates of older
workers.

Some understanding of the reasons for these problems may be
gained by examining the BLS methodology. The procedures used by the
BLS in making these projections have changed little over the last 20

years (Ryscavage, 1979). The basic strategy has been to extrapolate
past trends in labor force participation rates for various demographic (e.g., age, sex, race) groups into the future, and then to mul-
tiply these expected rates by projected population levels for these
groups to obtain an estimate of the size of the labor force for the
desired year. Projected population levels are regularly provided by
the Bureau of the Census, and since the number of births is quite
well known, estimating the number of adults up to 20 years in the
future is relatively easy, although unanticipated changes in mortality rates and especially net migration may cause some problems.

Estimating future trends in labor force participation rates is
more problematic, and is the major source of error in labor force
projections. As noted, the Bureau of Labor Statistics estimates
these future rates by the straightforward procedure of extrapolating
past trends in labor force participation rates.[2] The problem, of
course, is that the economic, demographic, social, and psychological
factors that produced recent trends may change. There are several
examples of such changes and the errors that they have caused in
labor force projections. The most obvious example is the unanticipated rise in the number of female participants in the last several
years produced by such factors as changes in sex-role attitudes,
increases in the age of first marriages, lower fertility rates,
higher divorce rates and/or an "added worker" effect--i.e., the declining labor market opportunities caused by the continued swelling
of the labor force by the baby boom cohort (e.g., Wachter, 1977).

Of even more relevance to our topic was the failure to foresee
the large increase in the number of young workers, particularly
students and females. For example, the BLS projected an increase in
the number of workers below the age of 35 between 1960 and 1975 of
14.8 million or 51.4 percent, while the actual increase was 19.0
million or 65.8 percent (Freeman, 1979). By simply extrapolating
previous trends, the BLS projections missed the shifts toward
greater labor force participation rates among young women and
students of both sexes.

Extrapolating labor force participation rates into the future
may be problematic for older individuals as well. The downward trend
in participation rates among those 55 and older has been variously
attributed to a decrease in the work ethic, mandatory retirement
rules, the increased availability of social security disability pensions, and probably most importantly, a rise in the level of retirement income (in particular social security and private pensions)
available to older individuals relative to the amount that they can

---

[2]These extrapolated trends are sometimes adjusted or tapered,
however, if the unadjusted trend implies an implausible rate at
some point in the future (Ryscavage, 1979).

earn by working. However, we may soon see a reversal in these
trends. The elimination or easing of mandatory retirement provisions
is the most obvious reason, although empirical research suggests that
relatively few workers are actually forced to retire against their
will or wish to continue working at their regular jobs beyond normal
retirement age (e.g., Parnes, 1981).

Perhaps more importantly, inflation, stagnant economic conditions, increased longevity, increasing numbers of older individuals,
declining dependency ratios, and the resulting financial strains on
pension funds and the social security system are likely to cause a
decrease in retirement income relative to expected standards of
living and potential earnings. Secularly increasing levels of education raise the opportunity costs (foregone earnings) of not working,
while increasing expectations of greater longevity (with the concomitant demands of saving for one's own, one's spouse's, and one's
parents' increased longevity) raise the need to work as well. Thus,
in the jargon of economists, substitution and income effects may both
operate to increase the labor force participation rates of older
workers in the decades ahead. If so, then the recent downward trend
in participation rates will be reversed and BLS estimates of the number of older workers by 1990 may well be too low.

Unfortunately, forecasting such changes and their effect on labor
force participation rates is an especially complex task, and it is
not entirely clear what would be the most effective approach to
modeling these changes. In a recent article in the Monthly Labor
Review, Ryscavage (1979) discussed the relative advantages of various
modifications of and alternatives to the present BLS approach. The
most promising, but perhaps also the most problematic, is the behavioral modeling approach. This approach would formally incorporate
behavioral models of labor supply, or the results of such models,
into labor force projection procedures. Typically, these models are
based on neo-classical economic theories of consumer choice, time
allocation, and human capital investments of individuals. They
generally express labor supply, or labor force participation, as a
function of the individual's wage opportunities (i.e., value of time
in the labor market), "shadow or reservation" wage (i.e., value of
time in non-labor market activities), unearned income and/or
variables believed to determine one's market wage, reservation wage,
and unearned income (e.g., education, labor force experience,
dependents, other family income, and local labor market conditions).

These models therefore provide a potential mechanism for modeling
the underlying effect of changes in social factors (e.g., increases
in education), economic factors (e.g., increases in wages and transfer payments), demographic factors (e.g., decreases in fertility),
and psychological factors (e.g., decreases in work ethic) on the
labor supply behavior of individuals, and, in turn, the labor supply
of aggregates. For example, the previous 15 years have been

characterized by increases in the number of younger adults compared with prime-aged and older adults, while the next 15 years will be characterized by an increase in the number of prime-aged adults relative to older and, especially, younger adults. Based on a relative income argument, Wachter (1977) has asserted that because of these changes in the relative <u>number</u> of adults of different ages, it would be incorrect to extrapolate recent trends in age-group specific labor force participation rates. He maintains that the influx of the baby boom cohort lowered the family income of young adults relative to their aspired standard of living. This has resulted in declining fertility and an increase in the likelihood of labor force participation, especially among secondary workers in the family, to reduce the discrepancy between actual and aspired family income. He argues further, however, that as the relative number of young adults decreases in the years ahead, their family income will rise relative to their aspirations. This will lower their incentive for work, leading to slower growth rates in participation among young adults. Wachter goes on to show that, relative to a simple extrapolation approach, a quantified version of his model predicts greater participation rates in the 1980s among older workers and lower participation rates among younger workers.

Despite their potential, serious questions remain as to whether the behavioral models developed to date actually represent fundamental or causal relationships regarding labor force participation and labor supply decisions. The important and difficult research tasks for the coming years are to demonstrate the superiority of conventional economic models over competing ones that derive from quite different causal mechanisms (e.g., theories in which social and psychological factors play a more important role relative to economic and demographic factors), especially in terms of their ability to predict the future. Unfortunately, behavioral models in economics have not yet proven themselves on these scores, and their estimates tend to be quite diverse. As Borjas and Heckman (1979) have summarized the findings to date: "The principal legend is that the empirical estimates of the same parameters obtained from the set of available studies display such diversity that they are of little use to policymakers."

Thus, despite the tremendous efforts and voluminous research of the past two decades on this subject, what Herbert Parnes (1970, pp. 32-33) wrote a decade ago still seems true today:

> On the theoretical level, the labor supply model originally suggested by Mincer and elaborated by others has proved to be a useful tool of analysis. . . Still, one ought not to exaggerate the achievements. On the theoretical side, although labor force decisions are thought to be collectively arrived at in order to maximize the utility of the family, no model has actually been able to reflect

this. Moreover, while the importance of "tastes" has been
acknowledged in all the research, very little has been done
to incorporate this variable--or more accurately, this complex of attitudinal variables--in the models that have been
used. As a consequence, the amount of variation among individuals that the models explain is very small indeed. . .
Second, a careful review of the recent literature on labor
force participation is an effective antidote for any unrealistic views one may hold about the magic of multiple
regression techniques. . . and the publication by sophisticated analysts of coefficients that are logically nonsensi-
cal are eloquent reminders of the complex and rigid mathematical assumptions that underly the use of the techniques.

For reasons such as these, and because of the persistent interest of policymakers in anticipating the responses of individuals to
a changing mix of social programs--e.g., welfare reform, unemployment insurance, social security, other forms of transfer payments,
etc.--enormous expenditures over the past decade have been made to
employ "random design experimental studies" of the likely effects of
alternative public policies. The obvious purpose is to assure that
subsequently observed differences in labor supply responses between
randomly selected experimental and control group subjects--beyond
those due purely to chance--are due to the program. This is because
the only logical differences between the two groups could occur as a
result of the program or chance differences in group assignment. In
the absence of a random design experiment, however, statistically
significant differences between the group which received the treatment and the comparison group may possibly be due to factors other
than the treatment. This empirical problem has confounded virtually
every past program evaluation and study of labor supply decisions.

Unfortunately, the results have hardly lived up to expectations.
First; random design experiments themselves are not without considerable faults, aside from their appreciable costs. For example, it is
quite difficult to estimate the effects of fertility decisions on
labor supply by way of a random design experiment. Secondly, they
too cannot prove cause-effect relationships, but merely document the
existence of correlations--oftentimes correlations based on too
narrow a sample to allow the results to be generalized more broadly.
Third, the results of random design experiments have themselves produced as wide a range of estimates of labor supply responses to
policy changes as the survey research they were designed to improve
upon. Borjas and Heckman (1979, p. 321) put the dilemma as follows:

If an "experiment" could be conducted that closely re-
sembled a proposed program, no (behavioral) model building
was (thought to be) required in order to assess the impact
of the program. As is evident from the literature this
hope was illusory. It is now clear, especially in the work

of Hausman and Wise, that experimental data require as much
and possibly more care in their analysis than do traditional data, in large part because of initial administrative decisions used to create samples and because of self-
selection decisions by experimental participants. It is
now widely recognized that the experiments did not and
could not directly estimate the likely impact of a widespread long-duration negative income tax. Like it or not,
we are stuck with the need for a model to interpret data
and to make policy forecasts.

These conclusions point to the need to expand our perspectives
on labor supply decisions. Perhaps more importantly, they point to
the need to expand our perspectives on all aspects of labor market
behavior. The next section of the paper deals with these issues and
the likely outcome.

Expanding Disciplinary Perspectives on Labor Supply Decisions and Models of Labor Market Behavior

While there has been some slight interest among economists
recently in incorporating social and psychological variables into
models of labor market behavior, the evidence generated thus far in
expanding disciplinary perspectives seems to be mixed. In the re-
mainder of this section we summarize the findings of these modest
efforts and draw implications for future research on labor market
behavior.

Edward Denison's (1979) studies, for example, have suggested
that work attitudes, motivation, and any erosion of the work ethic
have had little visible effects on recent trends in national levels
of productivity in this country. Furthermore, the longitudinal data
of economists from the University of Michigan's Panel Study of Income
Dynamics (PSID) have consistently shown "little evidence that individual attitudes and behavior patterns affect individual economic progress" (Duncan and Morgan, forthcoming). Using data from the first
five waves of the PSID, Morgan (1974) related changes in poverty
status, in total family income relative to needs, and in total tax-
able income of the household head and wife to a set of demographic
and work ethic type attitudinal data. Morgan (1974, p. 338) concluded that the social and psychological attitudes of individuals:

. . . affect almost none of the components of economic
status and their change over time. It is not merely that
these measures failed to show up for the entire sample of
families either by themselves or when other variables were
taken into account; they also failed to affect any of the
important subgroups of the population. Insofar as we have
segregated important subgroups, some of whom may have some
opportunities to make adjustments in their situations, the
negative evidence is impressive.

Similar conclusions were reached with data from the sixth and
seventh waves of the PSID (Lane and Morgan, 1975; Morgan, 1976),
wherein annual labor income of the household head, hourly earnings,
annual earnings, and total family income relative to needs were
studied. Furthermore, Duncan and Morgan (forthcoming) found no
relationships whatsoever between work ethic attitudes and growth
between 1971 and 1978 in hourly earnings, annual earnings, and
family income relative to needs for employed male heads of households. For female heads of households, there were no relationships
observed between a number of social and psychological attitudes and
1971-1978 growth in family income and family income/ needs (Duncan
and Morgan, forthcoming). Only Duncan and Hill (1975) observed any
evidence in the PSID data that work attitudes had any visible
effects on subsequent changes in economic status over the next five
years. These effects, however, were reported to be quite small.
Thus the major conclusions drawn from the PSID studies have been
that social and psychological variables have little bearing on labor
market behavior and thus their inclusion into economic models of
labor supply and labor market behavior would be to little avail.

Studies by economists using other micro data bases have led to
quite different conclusions, however. At a National Commission for
Manpower Policy conference reviewing findings from the National
Longitudinal Surveys (NLS), Arvil V. Adams (1976, pp. 74-75) concluded that NLS data:

> . . . have given strong support to the importance of atti-
> tudes in labor market behavior. Among these attitudes are
> the commitment to work and its relation to labor force
> participation; job satisfaction and its relation to inter-
> firm mobility; and initiative and its relation to earnings
> and other dimensions of labor market success . . . Among
> the most exciting contributions to policy made by longitu-
> dinal analysis are the findings concerning the importance
> of individual initiative, measured by the Rotter score.
> Not only have we learned that initiative pays off in the
> labor market, but also that individual initiative can be
> shaped by the opportunity structure present. Initiative
> therefore need not be considered exogenous by manpower
> policy, but instead, can be treated as endogenous subject
> to policy control.

Herbert Parnes' (1976, pp. 47-48) review of the major findings
from the NLS, reports that older workers with a strong work ethic
subsequently improved their employment situations more than older
workers who were ostensibly comparable in all regards except the
strength of their attachment to the dominant work ethic. Moreover,
such relationships were observed for black as well as white older
men, and for workers who remained with the same employer as well as
those who shifted jobs. Andrisani (1977) has shown the same sorts

of relationships for young black and white men as well. For young
women, Parnes (1976, pp. 47-51) also notes that their work ethics
measured before marriage are related to their labor force participation after becoming mothers years later. Strong relationships
between work ethic and subsequent willingness to retire early among
men in their forties and fifties have also been demonstrated with
NLS data (Parnes, 1976, pp. 47-51). Men who reported a weak work
ethic in 1966 were twice as likely to retire early by 1971, other
things statistically held equal, than comparable men with a strong
work ethic. Similarly, job dissatisfaction in 1966 was also
strongly associated with the likelihood of subsequent early retirement by 1971.

A recent book by Andrisani (1978) using NLS data has also produced a number of important findings about whether individuals'
attitudes toward work are eroding and whether such an erosion would
matter for the success of individuals in the labor market or in the
aggregate. His findings suggest that in the last decade job dissatisfaction began to increase from 5 to 13 percentage points among
each of the NLS cohorts. Extrapolating to the entire workforce,
this implies that about 10 million workers became less satisfied
with their jobs. Furthermore, the findings show that job dissatisfaction did not rise exclusively among those whose unique labor
market problems have already been singled out by policy makers for
special attention: the unskilled and poorly paid, and, in particular, minority group members faced with limited employment opportunities. Where job satisfaction has declined, the decline has not been
entirely at the lower end of the occupational, industrial, and
income structures, or primarily within certain age, sex, or race
groups.

Data from this study also provide evidence that job dissatisfaction has unfavorable labor market consequences--both for individuals
and in the aggregate, and particularly for youths. For example,
highly dissatisfied youths were from 18 to 42 percentage points more
likely than comparable youths who were highly satisfied with their
jobs to change employers subsequently. Moreover, since youths, and
black youths in particular, stand less to lose, the data not surprisingly show a stronger relationship between job dissatisfaction
and turnover among youths than older workers and among black youths
more so than whites. The evidence also suggests that job dissatisfaction imposes considerable costs on youths in terms of increased
unemployment, decreased labor force participation, and below average
growth in annual earnings. Yet the economic costs of job dissatisfaction reflect more than the costs of turnover which were borne
disproportionately by dissatified youths. Among comparable white
youths who did not change employers, there is considerable evidence
that those dissatisfied with their jobs were below-average in occupational and earnings advancement. Among those who changed employers, the dissatisfied were generally above-average in weeks of

unemployment as well. The evidence thus suggests that job dissatisfaction often leads to reduced productivity and to job changing that
has been less carefully planned than that which takes place among
comparable youths more highly satisfied with their jobs.

Other data from the same study provide further support for the
hypothesis that social and psychological variables are important
motivators of labor market behavior. Male youths with an "internal"
attitude--i.e., who perceive payoffs to hard work and initiative--
subsequently experienced greater labor market success than their
contemporaries who perceive less payoffs to their efforts. The
findings are consistent with those of The Coleman report (1966)
which found that differences in these same attitudes were a more
important factor in explaining educational achievement among black
youths than all of the differences in school quality and family
background combined. More specifically, the NLS data showed that
white and black young men with an internal outlook in 1968 were in
the better occupations and had higher hourly earnings two years
later than comparable youths with an external attitude. In the
analyses which came closest to estimating true causal relationships,
those examining subsequent growth in earnings and occupational
advancement, internals of both race groups were also more likely to
outdistance comparable externals in terms of both growth in hourly
earnings and occupational advancement.

As for the magnitude of the relationships, those young men who
were "slightly internal" in 1968 (a score of eight on the attitudinal measure) were estimated to have enjoyed a 12% differential in
hourly earnings two years later over comparable youths who were
"slightly external" in outlook (a score of twelve). Also, their
average hourly earnings were estimated to have advanced by $.20 per
hour more between 1968 and 1970 than the wage rates of comparable
youths who were "slightly external." The only aspect of labor
market experience examined that was not significantly related to
these work ethic type attitudes was growth in annual earnings.
Although the data did not address the issue directly, this may
reflect greater investments (foregone earnings) that youths with a
stronger work ethic and greater initiative have made in order to
realize their advantage two years later in hourly earnings and
occupational attainment. Greater investments in job search, mobility, and on-the-job training, in particular, may explain why youths
with a stronger work ethic outdistanced otherwise comparable youths
in growth in hourly earnings and occupational advancement without
exceeding their growth in annual earnings.

Differences among otherwise comparable youths in other social
and psychological variables--e.g., career ambition, expectations of
achieving career goals, commitment to work, attitudes toward one's
work role, attitudes toward the propriety of working mothers, and
spouse's attitude toward one's work role--were also shown in this

study to bear some relationship to <u>subsequent</u> labor market experience. In particular, young men with greater occupational ambition
advanced more in annual earnings over the next three years than
comparable youths who were less ambitious. Among the whites, their
occupational ambitions were also related to their degree of
occupational advancement, to advancement in hourly earnings, to the
reception of formal occupational training, and to fewer weeks of
unemployment. Among the black youths, the more ambitious were also
more inclined to receive formal occupational training, but there is
no evidence that they were more likely to advance occupationally or
in wage rates, or that they were any less likely to encounter
unemployment.

In addition, young men with greater self-confidence in their
ability to attain their occupational goals subsequently advanced
considerably more up the occupational ladder than otherwise comparable youths with less self-confidence. For example, their annual
earnings advancement over the next three years exceeded that of
those less confident by $825 to $1150, depending upon race, and the
more confident youths experienced three to four fewer weeks of unemployment as well. Among white young men, the more confident also
had considerably greater advancement in hourly rates of pay, fewer
weeks out of the labor force, and were more prone to be geographi-
cally mobile. Among women, those whose husbands were opposed to
their working were less likely in subsequent years to advance
occupationally or in earnings. They also encountered considerably
more unemployment, and were less likely than average to receive
formal training.

In addition to the NLS studies cited above, there are a few very
recent ones that tend to be consistent with those summarized here.
Becker and Hills (1980, 1981) for example, show that teenagers with
weaker work ethics have lower earnings and longer periods of <u>future</u>
unemployment (7 years later) than ostensibly comparable youths more
strongly committed to the work ethic; and that while young black men
have only slightly weaker work ethics than their white counterparts,
racial differences in their work ethic account for a substantial
portion of the racial differences in their unemployment. Hudis,
Hayward, and Macke (in press) found that young women's work ethics
affected their subsequent tendency to work, and their perceptions of
their husbands' attitudes about their working had a "surprisingly
strong impact" on their subsequent labor force participation and
fertility decisions as well. Statham and Larrick (1980) also found
that married women's work attachment and perceptions of their
responsibility in financially supporting their families are strongly
related to their subsequent earnings. Furthermore, Statham (1981)
found that married men participate less fully in the labor force
when they approve of women working, while married women participate
more fully when they approve of women working; and Shaw (1979)
reports that women's work ethic type attitudes and their disliking

for housework were systematically linked to their likelihood of
reentering the work force during the 1966–1977 period.

If these initial findings from the NLS, which as noted are
inconsistent with those from the PSID, are borne out by further
research, it would seem likely that nurturing the work ethic and
initiative of young people would facilitate the transition from
school to work, enhance subsequent career development, and promote
economic growth. Thus, expanding disciplinary perspectives in
research into labor market behavior would seem to offer considerable
promise for improving our understanding of the operation of labor
markets. The findings from the relatively few NLS studies on the
subject summarized here are all the more impressive since in virtually every case they use multivariate methods and longitudinal data
to demonstrate that the estimated effects of the social and psychological variables are neither reflecting the effects of background,
human capital, and demographic factors, nor reflecting the influence
of labor market experience on the social and psychological variables.

Indeed, there is reason to believe that these findings may understate the real effects of the attitudes on the labor market experience of individuals and in the aggregate, since it has not been
possible to isolate the indirect effects of the attitudes on labor
market experience via their effect on investments in education and
other forms of human capital. Nor has it been possible to estimate
the extent to which the effects of the attitudes are understated by
using such crude and simplistic, and thus inherently less reliable,
measures of social and psychological variables as are available in
the NLS.

Finally, another potentially important set of variables has also
received little attention by economists: namely, the role of institutional variables in shaping labor market behavior. Generally,
economists view these variables to be no more than the forms and
trappings whereby market forces are translated into reality (e.g.,
Doeringer and Piore, 1971). This view may be changing, however, as
the work of Nobel Laureate Herbert Simon and the realities of applied
research for public and private policymakers begin to trickle down
into the ranks of the various disciplines which are concerned with
labor market behavior. Let us now consider some other implications
of the changing age structure of the work force for labor market
research: namely, the labor market problems of youths and middle-aged
workers that are likely to occur in the years ahead.

Youth Labor Market Problems

Perhaps the most salient of all labor market issues in our
country over the last few years has been the employment problems of
youth. Since 1975, the unemployment rate for men and women in their
early 20s has hovered about 10 to 13 percent, and for teenagers, it

has been about 16 to 20 percent. Worse yet, for black teenagers unemployment rates have ranged from 30 to 40 percent and have recently
soared as high as 50 percent. Since these statistics represent the
highest measured levels of youth unemployment since the Great
Depression, they have generated considerable concern and much debate
over what remedial policies, if any, should be instituted.

Unfortunately, the usefulness and necessity of various policy
options are very difficult to assess because we lack a basic understanding of just what these statistics mean. For example, we do not
know exactly how much of a cyclical, structural, and/or frictional
imbalance between labor supply and labor demand is implied by these
statistics. Nor do we know how much hardship on youths or their
families is implied either in the short run or in the long run due to
unemployment early in careers. Still further, we do not know whether
these historically high rates are an unfortunate but transitory phenomenon or whether they represent more fundamental and long term problems for this and subsequent youth cohorts. Questions such as these
should be a primary focus of future research.

Perhaps the most fundamental research question, however, is the
following: To what degree will the aging of the baby boom cohort and
the coming of age of the baby bust cohort over the next 10 years lead
to lower unemployment rates among youth? Traditional economic theory
and common sense suggest that if younger and older workers are not
perfect substitutes for each other, then a decrease (increase) in the
proportion of young workers will lead to a decrease (increase) in the
unemployment levels of youth relative to the overall average unemployment rate, other things being equal. The results from recent
analyses of this issue are mixed, however. Wachter and Kim (1979)
used data from 1954 to 1978 and found evidence supporting the hypothesis, while Ragan (1977) used data from 1963 to 1972 and found no
supporting evidence. The results between cohort size and earnings
opportunities are less ambiguous: Studies by both Freeman (1980) and
Welch (1979) indicate that members of large cohorts suffer from
significantly lower earnings.

The primary conclusion to be drawn from such investigations as
these is that it is almost impossible to unambiguously separate the
effects of cohort size from several other competing factors--e.g.,
changes in the coverage and level of the minimum wage, the trend
toward increasing labor force participation among students, changes
in the draft and military enlistment programs, changes in labor
demand associated with the business cycle, government sponsored job
creation programs, changes in the availability and level of transfer
income (both in the form of cash and in-kind transfers), and last but
not least, secular changes in youths' attitudes toward work. These
analytical problems should not deter researchers, however, because
the relationship between relative cohort size and labor market opportunities is a pivotal issue determining the degree to which we can

expect newly entering cohorts to experience difficulties similar to current youth, and the degree to which the problems of the baby boom cohort will stay with them throughout their careers.

Additional questions must also be addressed if we hope to adequately explain previous trends in youth unemployment rates, forecast the future, and comprehend the meaning of youth unemployment rates. For example, is there a large reserve army of youth so discouraged by the lack of job opportunities that they have dropped out of the labor force altogether and thus are not counted as unemployed? An affirmative answer would imply that traditional unemployment rates understate the magnitude of youth unemployment problems both in terms of a disjuncture between supply and demand and possibly in terms of economic hardship for individuals and families as well. It would also imply a slower improvement in unemployment rates in the future, since these discouraged workers would likely reenter the labor force as labor market conditions improve.

Perhaps most importantly, what long-run effects on skill and career development will result from extensive periods of idleness during youth, from intermittent experience in dead-end jobs, and from secular declines in the quality of schooling? Some argue that unemployment during youth deprives an individual of valuable work and training experiences, produces discouragement, frustration, and decreased motivation, and/or serves as a negative screening device for employers, all of which lead to lower employment opportunities throughout the individual's work career. Others argue that, although unemployment is not necessarily a desirable state, it is frequently a period of effective job search activity resulting in a job that better fits the desires and capabilities of the individual, thus providing some long run benefit for an individual's career.

In this same vein, what portion of those who are counted as unemployed are only partially or casually attached to the labor market? Feldstein and Ellwood (1980), as well as others, argue that many of those youths who are unemployed either are students, or are looking for part-time work, and/or have only a weak desire to find work. In addition, it has been observed that almost all youth who are unemployed live at home. The apparent presumption here is that if a youth is at "home," his (her) earnings are not very important to the welfare of the household. While this may be true for most middle and upper class households, it is not true for many households that are below or near the poverty line. Nearly one-half of the almost 8 million unemployed workers in America are youths while an additional 25 percent are women over 25 years of age.

Answers to these questions require better labor force data. We need improvements in both the conceptualization and measurement of labor market behavior that more adequately capture varying degrees of attachment to the labor force, varying degrees of intensity of job

search, and minimum acceptable levels of both pecuniary and nonpecu-
niary job rewards for different individuals. This is consistent with
the recommendations of the National Commission on Employment and
Unemployment Statistics to collect better data on the qualitative
dimensions of labor market experiences (cf., Adams, 1981).

The importance of these questions and the development of several
longitudinal data files over the last few years have spawned several
empirical investigations into these issues (e.g., Becker and Hills,
1980; 1981; Ellwood, 1980; Stephenson, 1978). On balance, the evidence seems to suggest that teenage unemployment per se does not have
a long run "scarring effect." For example, Becker and Hills (1980)
found that young men who reported some unemployment as teenagers
averaged slightly higher earnings 8 years later than those who reported no unemployment. However, they also found that among those
with some unemployment, earnings were negatively related to the duration of teenage unemployment.

Perhaps the most reasonable tentative conclusion is that short
spells of unemployment during the teenage years are often a reflection of a useful adjustment to the labor market and effective job
search activity, while long spells of unemployment either are indica-
tive of, or help produce, employment problems throughout the individual's career. Regarding possible remedies, Becker and Hills
provided some evidence that public training programs and changes in
youths' work ethic may reduce the long run scarring effects of unemployment of long duration. Clearly, more definitive research along
these lines is essential in the years ahead.

To the extent that relative cohort size does influence relative
labor market opportunities, we can expect improved labor market
opportunities for the youth of 1990, other things being equal, and,
consequently, a lesser need for policy remedies for youth employment
problems. From other perspectives, however, a decrease in the number
of youths could also lead to new and different problems. In particular, concern may increase over the question, to paraphrase a recent
article in Time (June 9, 1980), "Who Will Fight for America?" I
doubt that this problem merits much concern. I recall that in 1936
the Oxford Union was passing resolutions that "we will not fight
another war for King and Country" and in 1939 all these young men
signed up promptly for military service. An obvious military threat
changes behavior dramatically. Of course, for another Vietnam, this
concern is justified. Even with today's relative glut of young
people, the military is finding it difficult to attract and retain
sufficient numbers of qualified people. As the relative number of
youth decreases, better information will be needed about the processes by which individuals decide whether to enlist and remain in
the military, and the role that military pay and benefit levels,
local labor market conditions, and patriotic values play in these
processes. In addition, a continued and more thorough examination of

the potential role of young women and young minorities in the military is warranted. These are but a few examples of the kinds of issues that should guide future research into the unique labor market problems of youth.

Prime Age Bulge: Career Problems for the Baby Boom Cohort

Not unlike the changes in physique that occur between youth and middle age, the bulge in the age distribution of the work force will inexorably shift toward the middle. As Table 1 indicates, the number of prime age workers will rise faster than the number of younger and older workers. Actually, the change can be pinpointed even more precisely. For male workers, the proportion between the ages of 35 and 44 will increase significantly over the next 10 years, while the proportion in each other age group will decline or stay about the same. For female workers, the 25 to 34 group, and especially, the 35 to 44 age group, will be the only ones showing significantly greater proportions between now and 1990. Later in the final decade of the century the aging of the baby boom cohort will cause the 45-54 year old age group to show the biggest increases. There are a number of implications of such age shifts in the work force for future labor market research.

Earlier we discussed the question of whether the decreasing relative size of the youth population would lead to an improvement in the labor market opportunities of youth. The other side of that question, of course, is whether the labor market problems that the baby boom cohort experienced during their youth will continue to plague them throughout their working careers. This may occur even if youth employment problems have no long term effects--e.g., if different individuals bear the brunt of an excess labor supply over different stages of the life cycle. As we argued above, more research needs to be focused on these questions as well as the more general issue of the relationship between cohort size and labor market opportunities.

Even among members of the smaller cohorts that now populate the prime age groups, the incidence of job loss and other career setbacks is far from trivial. For example, Parnes and King (1981) found that approximately one out of twelve middle-aged men had experienced an involuntary separation from a job after accumulating at least 5 years of seniority. A better understanding of the relationship between cohort size and labor market experiences is needed to anticipate the degree to which the incidence of such problems will increase with the aging of the baby boom cohort.

We also need better information about the form of these problems and how they are distributed among workers, as well as information about the processes determining the likelihood of such problems for individual workers. For example, will labor market problems be primarily in the form of depressed wages for all members of the cohort in general, or in the form of chronic unemployment for a small, but significant, minority? The answer to this question requires greater basic knowledge of how employers, workers, and unions respond to changes in labor market conditions. Hopefully, a better under-standing of these issues will be obtained so that appropriate policy remedies, if any, can be instituted as preventive measures, or if that is not successful or feasible, to alleviate the hardship caused by these problems.

We also need to know to what degree the incidence of labor market problems among mature workers is a function of (1) characteristics of the individual which they bring to the labor market, (2) early labor market experiences, and (3) more immediate demand factors as well as cohort size? Some evidence on this question is provided by Parnes and King (1981), who found that the loss of a long-service job is largely unrelated to important individual characteristics such as age, race, and education. And as we discussed above, despite a recent spate of empirical research on the topic, little is known with confidence about the effect of spells of unemployment and other labor market experiences early in the career on subsequent labor market success, although evidence does seem to favor the conclusion that early labor market experiences (e.g., youth unemployment) do not have significant long term effects.

Given our apparent inability to explain the occurrence of job losses among mature workers in terms of their individual characteris-tics and early labor market experiences, we need to ask ourselves whether our models are deficient or whether the incidence of job loss is mostly unrelated to these characteristics, perhaps dependent upon more immediate factors largely having to do with the competitiveness and viability of the firm? Such questions are extremely important given the deleterious and sometimes calamitous impact that such an experience can have on the economic and psychological well being of an individual and his or her family (cf., Parnes and King, 1981; Cobb and Kasl, 1977; Mick, 1975).

In this same vein, the aging of the baby boom cohort also implies increased attention to a relatively under-researched aspect of employment discrimination--that based on age. Questions of race and sex inequality may wane as researchers begin to explore age-related disadvantages of the men and women, whites and blacks, who soon will swell the ranks of those 40 and over.

The shift from large numbers of young workers to large numbers of prime-aged workers will also mean a more experienced work force. Moreover, it is likely that the increase in the amount of work exper-ience possessed by the average worker may be amplified by the recent increase in the labor force participation rates among young women, especially those with young children. Whereas middle-aged women in the labor force today have traditionally had only limited labor

market experience due to intermittent participation during their
childbearing years, increasing numbers of middle-aged women in the
decades ahead will have accumulated greater amounts of labor market
experience while their children were young.

Now that more than half of all working age women are in the labor
force, will the substantial increases in female labor force participation rates over the next 10-15 years projected on the basis of past
trends prove to be an over-statement? Will the steep rise in
families headed by females and the recently recognized phenomenon of
"displaced homemakers" receive the research attention that they
should in the years ahead? As the ranks of 25 to 44 year old women
swell in the years ahead, such problems as these should warrant much
greater empirical scrutiny. We also know that a very large proportion of poor children, and blacks in particular, live in single-
parent families, yet we know so little about the forces that have led
to such a sharp rise in the incidence of single-parent, female-headed
families in poverty. We know even less about the wisdom of various
alternatives for dealing with these sizable problems that one can
only expect to grow worse in coming years.

Furthermore, as more and more women move into their 30s and 40s,
their expectations for moving up the organizational ladder should
grow, while their problems in managing dual careers may grow like-
wise. Cherlin (1978), for example, argues that female employment and
career interests may be a cause as well as a consequence of divorce.
It is clear that individuals as well as society bear a large financial burden when marriages dissolve, especially within families with
young children. Shaw, (1979), for instance, found that 25 percent of
white women and over 40 percent of black women in their 30s and 40s
and not in poverty while married, fell into poverty when their
marriages ended. Too little is known about the relationships between
the managing of dual careers by women and the strains on so many
aspects of family life. Research in the decade ahead will no doubt
find these to be increasingly important concerns as the ranks of
middle-aged working women swell even more due to the aging of the
baby boom cohort.

To what degree will a more experienced and presumably more
skilled and stable work force imply a more productive economy? In
answering this question, it would be useful to determine whether the
decrease in the average experience level of American workers that
occurred during the late 1960s and 1970s was an important factor in
explaining the decline in productivity over the same period.
Although the literature suggests a considerable range of estimates,
including only trivial effects (e.g, Norsworthy, Harper, and Kunze,
1979), a majority of studies suggest that age and sex compositional
changes in the labor force have been a significant but not overriding
factor in explaining the decline in productivity over the last 15
years (Mark, 1979). Many conceptual and methodological issues remain

to be resolved, however, before we can be confident in any particular estimate of the size of this relationship.

One very important consideration that has not been adequately explored is the degree of synchronization between changes in the composition of the labor force and changes in the type of labor demanded. For example, during the last few years the increasing amounts of labor supplied by women has been accompanied by an increase in the demand for clerical and service type work which is typically considered to be female-type work. This "fit" between supply and demand is in one sense fortunate since it probably eased the absorption of women into the work force while helping employers find qualified workers.

On the other hand, the recent influx of young workers into the labor force was not accompanied by a corresponding increase in demand for inexperienced workers, thereby producing substantial youth unemployment and concern about reducing the minimum wage. In terms of the future, potential productivity increases that can result from a more experienced labor force may only be realized if there are concomitant changes in technology and the organization of work, thereby enabling employers to utilize the increased number of experienced workers. More generally, more research is necessary to identify future trends in the type of labor demanded that do not mesh with trends in the type of labor supplied. The Bureau of Labor Statistics' biennial Occupational Outlook Handbook is one of the few forays into this type of necessary research to date.

More experienced workers usually have accumulated greater amounts of skills and knowledge that is specific to their occupation, industry, and firm. However, the longer length of time since completion of formal education may imply a depreciation or obsolescence of general labor market skills. Of course, it may also imply a greater accumulation of firm, occupation, or industry specific skills. In addition, it implies a shorter working time horizon over which to reap the returns to additional investment in skill development, whether the investment is made by the worker or the employer. If the mature worker is in a job that is secure, then this greater amount of specific human capital is advantageous, and the possibly lower general human capital and shorter time horizon is not particularly problematic. However, if the enterprise becomes inviable because of inefficiencies or any other reason, then this shorter time horizon and lower level of general skills mean that the subsequent job loss can be detrimental and even catastrophic. As the labor force becomes more mature, the number of workers susceptible to such an event increases. Concomitantly, problems of mid-life crises, career changes, re-investments in education, reconciling dual careers, etc., will likely occur as well. These, too, are topics we are well advised to research carefully in the years ahead.

These social problems are likely to be made worse in the future by growth in developing countries that is likely to produce more competitive international trade. Thus, there will likely be even greater tension between the need to develop innovative productive processes and the need to provide employment security for a maturing workforce. Industrial democracy constitutes but one dimension of this tension. To the extent that workers are denied a voice in managerial decisions about plant closings as well as more general decisions affecting the competitiveness and viability of the firm, for instance, might they be provided with greater insulation from the potentially devastating effects on their careers and lives resulting from these decisions than are currently available--e.g., severance pay and extended unemployment insurance benefits in many cases? Or, if the firm and the government are not in a position to help displaced workers and they are supposed to look after themselves, should they at least have some say in managerial decisions?

Still further, because of their large numbers, members of the baby boom cohort, particularly those in the younger half, will likely confront reduced advancement opportunities in organizational and occupational hierarchies, as pyramidal hierarchies become swollen with stiff competition. This can be especially depressing and deflating because the reference group for the aspirations of the members of the baby boom chort is likely to be the earlier and much smaller cohort that preceded them with relatively clearer sailing up the organizational hierarchy. Further research into this area of career development is undoubtedly in order.

Finally, as the number of experienced workers increases over the next decade, quality of work life issues such as flexible work schedules, workplace autonomy, and health and safety may become increasingly important as well (Rosow, 1979). Much research is needed to better understand the relationship between various dimensions of worklife quality and job satisfaction and worker productivity. Such research should pay special attention to how these relationships may vary across individuals and jobs depending upon personality (e.g, need achievement) and social (e.g., family) situations, as well as organizational characteristics.

Summary of Major Points

(1) The most widely used labor force projections are those produced by the Bureau of Labor Statistics. These projections are problematic because of the practice of estimating future labor force participation rates by simply extrapolating recent trends into the future. A more behavioral approach is advocated since it theoretically provides a framework for modelling changes in the social, psychological, economic, and demographic factors that determine trends in labor force participation. In order for this to occur, labor market research must become more multidisciplinary and

interdisciplinary in its perspective in the years ahead. The limited
research to date suggests that this could be a fruitful area to
pursue in terms of improving upon conventional economic models of
labor supply and labor market behavior.

(2) The changes in the age structure of the population produced
by the aging of the baby boom cohort and the coming of age of the
baby bust cohort will be so dramatic over the next 10 years that
certain general changes in the age structure of the labor force will
occur even if there are unanticipated changes in labor force participation. First, the proportion of young workers will decrease substantially. Second, the proportion of prime aged workers, especially
in the 35-44 year old age group, will increase substantially. Third,
the proportion of older workers will remain about the same or decline
somewhat.

(3) A central issue involves the twin questions: (a) will the
changing age structure imply an easing of youth employment problems?
and (b) will the baby boom cohort continue to be plagued by a disproportionate share of labor market problems as they grow older--even if
there are no long run effects of youth unemployment? More generally,
the question is: does relative cohort size affect relative labor
market opportunities? Although the tentative answer is yes, much
more research is needed to investigate the degree to which the size
of this effect varies across different segments of the labor market
and over different stages of the life cycle and time periods.

(4) Those members of the baby boom cohort who experienced moderate amounts of unemployment as youths do not appear to be disadvan-
taged relative to those who experienced no unemployment in terms of
long-run career opportunities. However, those who experienced long
and/or frequent spells of unemployment will probably be more likely
than others to suffer labor market problems throughout their careers.
Whether this is due to the unemployment itself, or whether the long
and frequent spells of unemployment are symptoms of underlying problems awaits the outcome of further research.

(5) It is likely that serious problems exist with using unemployment as a measure of either an imbalance between supply and demand in
the labor market or economic hardship. More generally, we need
improvements in both the conceptualization and measurement of labor
force data that more adequately captures varying degrees of attachment to the labor force and varying degrees of intensity of job
search. We also need to know much more about the cyclical, structural, and frictional aspects and long run effects of youth
unemployment.

(6) Will a more experienced and presumably more skilled and
stable work force lead to a more productive economy? The answer will
partly depend upon the degree to which changes in technology and the

organization of work will allow for the utilization of greater numbers of mature, stable, and experienced workers.

(7) Involuntary job loss can have a severe and even catastrophic effect on the career and life of a mature worker and his or her family. Unless corrective action is taken, the incidence of such a job loss may increase because of the combination of increasing numbers of mature workers and increasing pressure from foreign competition which can force a firm to modify its productive processes in ways that disproportionately eliminate the jobs of older workers.

(8) As they mature, the members of the baby boom cohort may face reduced opportunities for advancement up organizational hierarchies relative to smaller birth cohorts. This may be especially true for those born in the latter half of the baby boom cohort, who will almost always find a very high concentration of only slightly older workers ahead of them in the promotion queue.

(9) The large influx of dual career oriented women in the years ahead poses numerous research and policy challenges. Specifically, the strains of managing dual careers may have lasting consequences for families and society as well, yet so little is known to date about the dynamic forces which produce these strains and their aftermath.

(10) Finally, problems of age discrimination in employment may begin to rival race and sex-based forms of labor market inequality in the decades ahead, as the men and women, whites and minorities from the baby boom cross the legally protected threshold of age 40.

References

Adams, A. V. Lessons from the national longitudinal surveys: A commentary. Current Issues in the Relationship Between Manpower Research and Policy. Washington, DC: National Commission for Manpower Policy, Special Report No. 7, March 1976, 72-79.

Adams, A. V. The American work force in the eighties: New problems and policy interests require improved labor force data. The Annals of the American Academy of Political and Social Sciences, 453, January 1981, 122-129.

Andrisani, P. J. Internal-external attitudes, personal-initiative, and the labor market experience of white and black men. Journal of Human Resources, 1977, 12, 308-328.

Andrisani, P. J. Work attitudes and labor market experience. New York: Praeger Publishers Inc., 1978.

Becker, B. E., & Hills, S. M. Teenage unemployment: Some evidence of the long-run effects on wages. Journal of Human Resources, 1980, 15, 354-372.

Becker, B. E., & Hills, S. M. Youth attitudes and adult labor market activity. Industrial Relations, 1981, 20, 60-70.

Borjas, G., & Heckman, J. Labor supply estimates for public policy
    evaluation. Proceedings of the Thirty-First Annual Meeting.
    Madison: Industrial Relations Research Association, 1979,
    320-331.
Bureau of Labor Statistics, Occupational Outlook Handbook.
    Washington, D.C.: U.S. Government Printing Office, 1981.
Cherlin, A. Employment, income, and family life: The case of
    marital dissolution. Women's Changing Roles at Home and on the
    Job. Washington, D.C.: National Commission for Manpower Policy
    Special Report, 1978, 26, 157-180.
Cobb, S., & Kasl, S. Termination: The consequences of job loss.
    Washington, D.C.: NIOSH, U.S. Department of HEW, 1977.
[The] Coleman report: Equality of educational opportunity.
    Washington, D.C.: U.S. Government Printing Office, 1966.
Denison, E. Accounting for slower economic growth. Washington,
    D.C.: The Brookings Institution, 1979.
Doeringer, P., & Riore, P. Internal labor markets and manpower
    analysis. Lexington: D.C. Heath and Co., 1971.
Duncan, G., & Hill, D. Attitudes, behavior patterns, and economic
    outcomes: A structural equations approach. In G. Duncan and J.
    Morgan (Eds.), Five thousand American families -- Patterns of
    economic progress, 2nd ed. Ann Arbor: The University of
    Michigan, Institute for Social Research, 1975.
Duncan, G., & Morgan, J. Sense of efficacy and subsequent change in
    earnings -- a replication. Journal of Human Resources, in
    press.
Ellwood, D. Teenage unemployment: Permanent scars on temporary
    blemishes. The youth employment problem - Dimensions, causes,
    and consequences. Washington, D.C.: Youth Knowledge
    Development Report 2.9, U.S. Government Printing Office, 1980.
Feldstein, M., & Ellwood, D. Teenage unemployment: What is the
    problem? The Youth employment problem - Dimensions, causes, and
    consequences. Washington, D.C.: Youth Knowledge Development
    Report 2.9, U.S. Government Printing Office, 1980.
Flaim, P., & Fullerton, H. N. Labor force projections to 1990:
    Three possible paths. Monthly Labor Review, 1978, 101, 25-35.
Freeman, R. B. The effect of demographic factors on age: Earnings
    profiles. Journal of Human Resources, 1979, 14, 289-318.
Fullerton, H. N. The 1995 labor force: A first look. Monthly
    Labor Review, 1980, 103, 11-21.
Hudis, R., Hayward, M., & Mache, A. A longitudinal model of
    sex-role attitudes, labor force participation, and childbearing.
    Journal of Marriage and the Family, in press.
Lane, J., & Morgan, J. Patterns of change in economic status and
    family structure. In G. Duncan and J. Morgan (Eds.), Five
    thousand American families -- Patterns of economic progress (2nd
    ed.). Ann Arbor: The University of Michigan, Institute for
    Social Research, 1975.
Mark, J. A. Productivity trends and prospects. In C. Kerr and J.
    M. Rosow (Eds.), Work in America: The decade ahead. New York:
    Van Nostrand Reinhold, 1979.

Mick, S. Social and personal costs of plant shutdowns. Industrial
    Relations, 1975, 14, 203-208.
Morgan, J. Change in global measures. In J. Morgan, et al. (Ed.),
    Five thousand American families -- Patterns of economic progress
    (1st ed.). Ann Arbor: The University of Michigan, Institute
    for Social Research, 1974.
Morgan, J. A seven year check on the possible effects of attitudes,
    motives and behavior patterns on change in economic status. In
    G. Duncan and J. Morgan (Eds.), Five thousand American families
    -- Patterns of economic progress (4th ed.). Ann Arbor: The
    University of Michigan, Institute for Social Research, 1976.
Norsworthy, J. R., Harper, M., & Kunze, K. The slowdown in
    productivity growth: Analysis of some contributing factors.
    Brookings Papers on Economic Activity, 1977, 387-422.
Parnes, H. S. Labor force participation and mobility. A review of
    industrial relations research (1st ed.). Madison: Industrial
    Relations Research Association, 1970, 1-78.
Parnes, H. S. The national longitudinal surveys: Lessons for human
    resource policy. Current issues in the relationship between
    manpower research and policy, Washington, D.C.: National
    Commission for Manpower Policy Special Report No. 7, March 1976,
    25-71.
Parnes, H. S. The retirement experience. In H. S. Parnes, et al.
    (Eds.), Work and retirement: Longitudinal studies of men.
    Cambridge: MIT Press, 1981.
Parnes, H. S. and King, R. The incidence and impact of job loss
    among long service workers. In H. S. Parnes et al. (Eds.), Work
    and retirement: Longitudinal studies of men. Cambridge: MIT
    Press, 1981.
Ragan, J. Minimum wages and the youth labor market. The Review of
    Economics and Statistics, May 1977, 59, 129-136.
Rosow, J. Quality of life issues for the 1980s. In C. Kerr and J.
    Rosow (Eds.), Work in America: The decade ahead. New York:
    Van Nostrand Reinhold, 1979, 157-187.
Ryscavage, P. BLS labor force projections: A review of methods and
    results. Monthly Labor Review, 1979, 102, 15-22.
Shaw, L. Changes in the Work Attachment of Married Women, 1966-
    1976. Columbus: The Ohio State University, Center for Human
    Resource Research, 1979.
Shaw, L. Economic consequences of marital disruption. Women's
    changing roles at home and on the job. Washington: National
    Commission for Manpower Policy Special Report No. 26, September
    1978, 181-204.
Smith, R. E. Projecting the size of the female labor force: What
    makes a difference? In C. Lloyd, E. Andrews, and C. Gilroy
    (Eds.), Women in the labor market. New York: Columbia
    University Press, 1979.
Statham, A. Women's propensity to work and share support responsi-
    bility: Implications for the labor force behaviors of married
    men and women. Columbus: The Ohio State University, Center for
    Human Resource Research, 1981.

Statham, A., & Larrick, D. Perceived responsibility for the
    family's financial support and women's occupational success.
    Columbus: The Ohio State University, Center for Human Resource
    Research, 1980.
Stephenson, S. The transition from school to work with job search
    implications. Youth unemployment: Its measurement and meaning.
    Washington, D.C.: U.S. Department of Labor, ETA, 1978, 65-86.
Sum, A. Female labor force participation: Why projections have
    been too low. Monthly Labor Review, 1977, 100, 18-24.
Time, Who will fight for America? June 9, 1980.
Wachter, M. Intermediate swings in labor force participation.
    Brookings Papers on Economic Activity, 1977, 2, 545-576.
Wachter, M. & Kim C. Time series changes in youth joblessness.
    National Bureau of Economic Research Working Paper No. 384.
Welch, F. Effects of cohort size on earnings: The baby boom
    babies' financial bust. Journal of Political Economy, 1979, 87,
    565-597.

POSTSCRIPTS AND PROSPECTS

Ross Stagner

Wayne State University

Detroit, MI

Before commenting on the preceding papers specifically, I would like to define my own frame of reference. I am concerned about the impact of the changing age distribution of the American labor force on identifiable groups of human beings. These groups are, first, the workers themselves. We can anticipate -- indeed, we can observe -- conflicts between younger and older workers. We need to concern ourselves with the effects of forced retirement. The paper by Andrisani and Daymont reminds us that it is too early to exert major efforts on behalf of the elderly employee. Right now we have an up-surge in the so-called "prime age" category of workers, and this may have undesirable consequences for both the very young and the older persons in the work force. But we must also be concerned with plan-ning for two decades hence, when the elderly will begin to comprise a major percentage of the work force.

It is rather easy, in looking at such problems, to conceptualize them primarily in terms of employment policy; that is, to delegate to managers the decision-making with regard to who gets hired, trained, promoted, transferred, and retired. This may not be a good idea; it is clear that union officials are demanding some voice in these decisions even today. Government officials are also demanding a voice in these matters, as evidenced by the restrictions on com-pulsory retirement.

Union leaders are also faced with intra-union problems related to the age composition of their membership. Questions of immediate wage gains versus retirement benefits, health insurance, etc., are already divisive influences, pitting the young against the old. We ought to give some thought to future developments in this area.

47

Finally, it is proper to give some thought to the impact on the welfare of the entire population, who may be categorized as consumers for this purpose. How far can we go in devising policies which protect one or another of the age groups of workers without having an adverse impact on the general welfare? In my remarks, I shall play back and forth between these various reference groups while commenting on the remarks of Andrisani and of Sheppard.

Postscripts

Andrisani has presented data which call for a shift in emphasis, at least in my viewpoint, with regard to age-related problems. I had been under the impression that "the graying of the American work force" was already upon us. The Andrisani projections are quite persuasive in indicating a need to focus in this decade on the "prime age" group (35-44). In the 1990s we must take steps to insure, in the following decade, that we are prepared to cope with an expansion of the elderly component of the working population.

As I expect to demonstrate shortly, we shall need this extra time interval to plan and experiment with procedures which will ease the problems of an aging work force and minimize the adverse impact on the consuming public. The extra time Andrisani offers us should not become an excuse for deferring consideration of potential problems. I shall therefore offer some specific suggestions with regard to the question of the older employee, in the hope that field experiments will be initiated to obtain information on suitable procedures.

Andrisani and Daymont have also pointed out a probable increase in the female component of the work force. Since the topic has been assigned to another panel, I shall not comment further on it here.

Let me now mention a few specific points I found interesting in Andrisani's presentation. As a psychologist interested in economic theory, I wish to express approval of what he called "behavioral modeling" in the forecasting of labor supply. Far too much of economic theorizing in recent years has sounded like "How many angels can dance on the head of a pin?" There is a familiar joke about the economist shipwrecked on a desert island. A case of canned food floats ashore, without a can opener. How does the economist solve his problem? He assumes the presence of a can opener. This kind of contrary-to-fact thinking has been all too prevalent in academic publications and in advice to governmental officials. Behavioral modeling sounds as if some economists are trying to relate their conceptualizations to the actions of real human beings.

Let me also thank Andrisani for a compact summary of data relating psychological variables, attitudes, and motives, to labor

market participation. While industrial psychologists have long
investigated such variables, their researches have tended to be on
small populations with limited possibilities for generalization. I
can foresee a fruitful collaboration of industrial psychologists
with this new kind of economist.

Let me turn now to a consideration of some specific issues which
seem to me to be crucial to understanding trends in industrial
management and worker behavior. Andrisani and Sheppard have both
commented on the rebellious attitudes of young, vigorous, tolerably
well-educated workers toward fragmented, repetitive jobs, such as
assembly-line work. Industry has been responding to this development by studying job redesign and restructuring the work arrangement
in factories and offices. However, it seems to me that we need more
concern with the entry-level employee, and especially with trying to
develop job commitment in these young workers. Research on these
lines might contribute to a stable work force ten or twenty years
hence.

My remarks will be somewhat different from those I would have
presented had the projections indicated that a sizeable shift toward
the upper age grouping would occur by 1990. This is of course only
a matter of emphasis. Fair and judicious treatment of workers at
all age levels is still necessary; and new procedures may be needed
only to the extent that factory and office technologies have not
been modified to suit the needs of human beings.

The Andrisani data indicate that in the immediate future we
shall have a relative shortage of younger, entry-age workers, an
increase in the so-called "prime" group, and perhaps a slight
decrease in the older age group. I interpret this to mean that at
least some of our concerns about unemployment in the young adult
population will be alleviated; it also suggests that far-sighted
employers will be making an extra effort to recruit young applicants
to forestall shortages a decade hence.

Andrisani asks, "Will a more experienced and presumably more
skilled and stable work force lead to a more productive economy?"
In the following pages I shall suggest some managerial policies
which may encourage an affirmative answer to that question, but I
should note that I do not consider the age of the work force to be
an important determinant of productivity. The quality of the tools
-- the technology of production -- is much more important. Nevertheless, at any given state of technology, the behavior of the
workers does indeed have some relevance, and I shall operate on that
assumption.

Concern about the age of the work force has taken two radically
different forms. One, a vigorous lobbying effort, has resulted in
the passage of ADEA--pushing back the age of compulsory retirement.
This would seem to predict an increasing percentage of older workers

on the job. However, the data do not confirm this. The second
factor, diametrically opposed, is the demand of the workers for
earlier retirement. Empirical studies show that this force is
winning out. Table 1 indicates that in a large public utility,
managerial and nonmanagerial employees alike seem to be electing
retirement at ages far below compulsory retirement. This, further,
is in an industry not noted either for high managerial stress or for
excessive strain on lower level workers.

The nub of the early retirement problem, as seen from a
psychologist's point of view, is to be found in the managerial
belief that older employees are less productive. This belief is
probably complex, and may include either an emphasis on declining
speed and accuracy of performance, or on the higher costs of more
senior employees who might be replaced with younger individuals at
the bottom of the salary scale. At any rate, many companies are
offering financial incentives for early retirement, and these
incentives are indeed altering the age composition of their
establishments, as illustrated by Table 2.

The policy of encouraging early retirement runs head on into an
issue which has received considerable attention from Dr. Sheppard,
that of the "dependency ratio." This ratio is computed by determining the proportion of productive workers to the total population,
although it has been popularized recently by focusing on the ratio
of productive workers to those on retirement or unemployed. The
dependency ratio is implicated in the general problem of inflation,
since a decrease in output of goods and services, with consumption
steady or increasing, constitutes an inflationary pressure. In this
large frame of reference, it would seem good social policy to
encourage older people to stay in productive employment, and ques-
tionable for the individual employer to encourage early retirement.
This, of course, contradicts the manager's concern with optimum
profitability for his/her enterprise.

The central psychological phenomenon in this array of problems
is, curiously enough, the phenomenon of perception. Managers

Table 1. Mean Retirement Age of Managerial and Nonmanagerial
          Employees 1975 – 1980 (Data from a large public utility)

	Managerial	Nonmanagerial
1975	57.62	59.72
1976	56.43	60.13
1977	56.25	60.15
1978	57.14	58.10
1979	57.70	57.20
1980	58.50	58.20

Table 2. Effect of Special Incentives for Early Retirement: Mean
          Retirement Age (Data from a major oil company)

	Incentive Offered	No Incentive Offered
1975	54.2	60.2
1976	57.9	60.0
1977	57.7	59.6
1978	57.8	60.0
1979	57.1	59.7
1980	57.1	60.3

perceive older employees as less productive, more prone to
accidents, more likely to have sizeable medical costs, and so on.
Also, they tend to get higher pay for the same job, as compared to
younger people. Thus the manager sees his task as that of
facilitating the departure of the older worker, as he believes it
will favor profitability of his enterprise.

Are these perceptions accurate? Managers, workers, and union
officials tend to share this stereotype of the older worker as less
productive. Curiously enough, there is very little evidence, and
most of it is contradictory. Of seven recent research papers I
located, only two could be interpreted as supporting the stereotype
of the elderly as slower or less efficient; two showed the older
group to be somewhat superior, and three concluded that no significant difference existed.

The problem, however, is more intricate than simply reporting
performance ratings by supervisors, as virtually all of these
studies did. If a supervisor believes in the stereotype of the
older worker as slower and less efficient, he will pick up bits of
evidence to support this belief, and will ignore contradictory
information. Curiously enough, many older employees share the same
stereotype. So, in an appraisal interview situation, they may agree
with judgments that, "I am slowing down a bit" or "I am not as
vigorous as I was five years ago." The result may be a self-
fulfilling prophecy in which a decline in performance ratings leads
to an actual reduction in effectiveness.

Some of this problem derives from the fact that most time-study
experts seem unable to agree with each other regarding work performance. In one relevant study, Lifson (1953) found that six experts,
including two professors of industrial engineering, disagreed on
simple ratings of speed of work. Pursell et al. (1980) correlated
five tests expected to predict work performance with performance
ratings and got figures close to zero. However, after intensive
training of the supervisors in how to judge performance, the

validity figures jumped markedly. The conclusion, inevitably, is
that estimates of declining performance of elderly workers are
suspect until it can be shown that those making the ratings can
agree with each other and with objective indices of output.

I cannot leave this question of the stereotype of older workers
as less efficient without pointing a finger of blame at many
researchers in the field of gerontology. Well over half the
articles comparing older and younger workers on ability or
performance conclude with generalizations based on mean differences:
"The average output of the younger workers was 20% greater" or "The
reaction time of the older workers was 15% slower." These sweeping
generalizations ignore the wide range of individual differences in
both age groups. It is much more appropriate to conclude with a
statement such as "The median of the older group was exceeded by 65%
of the younger workers" or "20% of the older group performed better
than the average in the young group." Such conclusions remind the
reader that many older employees are equal or superior to many in
the younger categories. I am in complete agreement with the comment
by Sheppard (1970) that far too many investigators have "a tendency
to derive averages only, which frequently obscures the exceptions
and deviants from the median...and thus affects on a very practical
level the lives of individual men and women" (pp. 6-7).

These beliefs and stereotypes about older employees have
considerable significance for the operations of industry. The
beliefs of managers determine the hiring opportunities for older
applicants, the chances of re-training for older employees when
technological change occurs, promotions for older workers, and so
on. The operation of age-discriminatory stereotypes in hiring has
been demonstrated by numerous studies, e.g., Rosen and Jerdee (1976)
and Craft et al. (1979). Descriptions of applicants, identical
except for age, were given to managers and they were asked to rate
employability. There was a significant tendency to discriminate
against workers over 55, sometimes even over 50. Recommendations
for retirement were also affected by age in such experiments (cf.
Rosen, Jerdee, and Lunn, 1980). Given identical descriptions of job
performance for two employees, immediate retirement is recommended
more often for the older individual.

The observations cited so far indicate that employers tend to
hold negative stereotypes of older employees, and that management
decisions adverse to the employee are affected by these perceptions.
I should note that workers themselves often agree with the
stereotype, and older workers are often more severe than younger
persons in judging the errors made by older individuals (cf.
Mullick, 1981). Interestingly, union officials seem to be less
susceptible to this error, although systematic data are not common.
Fritz (1978) comments that union leaders are more accurate than
employers in judging reasons for retirement, and more supportive of

retraining for older employees. Unions, of course, have emphasized seniority as evidence of qualification for higher-level jobs, mainly to block favoritism by supervisors, and so it is in a sound union tradition to oppose compulsory retirement. At the same time -- responding to worker demand -- the unions have campaigned success- fully for early retirement opportunities, and, as the data cited above indicate, workers have taken advantage of these contract provisions in large numbers.

Prospects

Studies of ability and aging. There is a voluminous literature on the change of sensory, perceptual, cognitive, and motor abilities with age. I cannot review it here, but will only develop a few important points. First, as Baugher (1978) concluded, the picture of changing abilities over time is complicated and the data are often inconsistent. Speed of motor response seems to be one measure on which declines are commonly found, but even here, the overlap of older with younger distributions is substantial. Owens (1966) and Horn and Cattell (1967) have assembled data indicating that loss of intellectual ability with age is by no means universal or uniform. In some cases individuals have actually shown increases in test performance between 60 and 70.

More important is the fact that different motor, sensory and cognitive functions mature and decline at different rates. Thus, as McFarland (1973) emphasized, we need to determine the functional age for each of various functions. A person who may have lost the ability to perform one job efficiently may still be normal or better with respect to the abilities required for another job. These should not be combined into a single measure of the individual's Functional Age on the analogy of Binet's Mental Age, because, as we have learned long since, analysis of mental age into primary mental abilities provides a much better guide to vocational planning, remedial instruction, and so on.

McFarland (1973) also stressed the idea that individuals develop compensatory skills or strategies which bypass a deteriorated function. Thus, a person with diminished hearing may arrange his work situation so that visual signals provide the information he needs. I think McFarland was excessively optimistic in his assertion that "compensation takes place for every decline, and if certain capacities are diminished, others are enhanced" (quoted by Sheppard and Rix, 1977, p. 74.) This is scarcely defensible; many oldsters have failed to develop compensatory skills. Nevertheless, it merits consideration by reminding us that not every loss is fatal.

McFarland (1973) also pioneered in advocating a profile method of matching workers with jobs, especially at advanced ages. He

reminded us that "...essentially all persons are at the same time
suited for some activities, while unsuited or unfit for others."
Meier and Kerr (1976) give more details on a profile-matching method
called GULHEMP, in which fitness ratings are developed for the
individual on seven attributes, and jobs are classified on the same
seven requirements. Thus the individual who is deficient in one
respect may still find a job where he meets the requirements for
effective functioning. Evidence that profile matching increases job
satisfaction has been reported by Phillips et al. (1978).

Discrimination has also been reported against elderly workers
when retraining for new technology is being planned. It is
therefore relevant to note that a variety of studies show that the
learning disadvantage of the worker over 60 is slight or non-
existent. Particularly, if older employees are permitted to work at
their own pace, they usually achieve the same level of accuracy and
production as their younger co-workers. Some studies indicate that
programmed instruction helps older workers raise their speed of
learning to the level of younger groups, and others cite the value
of the "discovery" method (Belbin, 1965). Goldstein (1980)
criticizes the literature on training as relying too heavily on
laboratory procedures and using material not job-related. We really
know very little about age effects on re-training for workers faced
with new technologies.

Re-training is necessary in part because of the rapid obsolescence of knowledge and skills. Dubin (1972) has claimed that many
professionals are obsolescent five or at most ten years after completion of training. If true, this would no doubt reinforce managerial attitudes favoring young employees. However, some observers
believe that this obsolescence has been grossly exaggerated. It is
quite likely that what is missing is a bit of the most advanced
technology, of the very latest developments in engineering or
accounting or law or medicine. For most jobs, it is probable that
intimate acquaintance with this up-to-the-minute material is not
absolutely necessary. Regardless of the alleged obsolescence of
skills, Price et al. (1975) found that "the high performers (engineers) in the 40-year age group and the 50-plus age group have
higher average ratings than do the middle and low performers in the
younger age groups." This would indicate that it would be a
grievous error to discriminate against older engineers merely
because they were surpassed by the very best of the younger group.
Further, it would seem that older employees could be kept up to date
by occasional refresher courses, although Price et al. noted that
performance ratings seemed unrelated to participation in such
continuing education programs.

Job satisfaction. Another aspect of aging which merits brief
mention is that of job satisfaction. Employers have been alarmed by
a rise -- modest but generally visible -- in the level of dissatis-

faction of workers in the last decade. Job dissatisfaction is
important in relation to production and costs because it correlates
substantially with absenteeism and turnover. Both factors tend to
add to costs and hence to inflation.

In general, the research data indicate that if employers want
satisfied workers, they should keep on the older group and minimize
the proportion of younger employees. Studies showing older workers
to be more contented have been reported by Caplan et al. (1975),
Stagner (1975), Sheppard and Herrick (1972), Quinn and Shepard
(1974), and Phillips et al. (1978), to cite only a sample.

A more interesting question may be: Why are older workers more
likely to report job satisfaction? Answers include: selective out-
migration (discontented workers quit), selective transfer within the
firm (union contracts often allow senior employees to bid on more
interesting jobs), habituation (unpleasant stimuli become less
noticeable with time), and feelings of control (over time the worker
may become more secure and self-confident that he/she can cope
effectively, and so feel more satisfied). No doubt there are other
possibilities, but these are obvious.

There may also be increasing discontent with specific aspects of
employment as age increases. Muchinsky (1978) presented data
indicating that "the work itself" was more satisfying to older
workers, but prospects for pay and promotion improvements were less
satisfying. Given the degree of bias against older workers we have
already noted, the feeling of these employees that prospects for
higher pay and promotion looked gloomy was merely a realistic
perception. Saleh and Otis (1963) reported that older workers who
enjoyed "the work itself" were less willing to retire, while those
mentioning pay or surroundings sought early retirement.

Mid-Life Career Change. People may "retire" or change careers
after having been successful in one profession or another.
Considerable attention has been given recently to the phenomenon of
"burn-out" or loss of interest in even a highly-paid, challenging
profession such as medicine. Sarason (1977) believes that this
problem is of increasing importance, and suggests that the frequency
with which middle-aged individuals drop out of an occupation for
some totally different activity will rise.

Does this phenomenon have anything to do with aging? In a
certain sense it must, since one must reach a certain age to be
characterized as middle-aged. There is considerable doubt that it
is a function of chronological age, since younger males and females
are now found to abandon their jobs and undertake new ventures.
What is perhaps most clearly relevant is that the career change
rarely occurs in people beyond 60, and this is hardly surprising,
since the time available for development of skill and demonstration
of achievement is perceived as small.

Mid-life career change is related to industry in the sense that many careers are described as boring; many jobs are "dead end" affairs; even professionals view their daily activities as mechanical repetitions of meaningless performances. As Sarason (1977) says of the "burnt-out" professional, "this educated elite, younger and older, may well be finding their work and career sources of disappointment" (p. 97). The mid-career change, then, may be considered as an expression of frustration, of dissatisfaction with the prior career choice, and a last chance to try for another, more satisfying style of life. In that respect it clearly is part of the problem of aging; Sarason even argues that it reflects an unconscious desire to postpone death. The new undertaking is viewed, he holds, as a revitalizing experience and a new opportunity for self-actualization before life ends.

The significance of the increased frequency of such mid-career shifts probably is to be found in motivation. Young people take jobs partly to demonstrate maturity and independence of parents, but also to obtain funds to purchase food, clothing, shelter and other basic necessities. However, in our affluent society, these survival needs are easy to satisfy, and according to current theory, ego motives such as prestige-seeking and self-actualization come into play. Now modern industry is poorly structured to satisfy such needs (this is a fundamental problem with satisfying young, relatively well-educated industrial workers). No one is greatly surprised if an auto assembly worker changes from his factory job to one in selling, or running a hunting lodge, or driving a truck. We are surprised when physicians, lawyers, dentists and accountants abandon comfortable practices for jobs as bartenders, farmers, or construction workers. The explanation which seems most plausible is that these persons, having achieved a secure economic base, feel free to do something different, and to escape from perceived constraints. It will be instructive to follow up some of these dramatic cases after ten years and ascertain how many have returned to the earlier occupation.

A complementary phenomenon is reported by Clopton (1978), who also studied mid-career changes. He concentrated on a group dissatisfied with routine jobs who went back to college and trained for a professional or technical career. Thus, job satisfaction may precipitate change, but the direction of change will be determined by ability and opportunity. At any rate, it seems clear that mid-life career changes will become a more important part of the American economy, with increasing confusion for those who try to predict the distribution of the population in jobs ten years hence.

Very early retirement. A somewhat analogous phenomenon is also worth considering, if only because Dr. Glickman specified "lifestyle" as one of the variables to be considered here. I refer to a job-change which I call VER (very early retirement) because it

occurs long before age 62. VER is characterized by dropping out of
the so-called "rat race" and living off of relatives, friends, food
stamps, and welfare. Lefkowitz (1979) has documented the phenomenon
in some detail. The persons he interviewed were unanimous in that
they owed nothing to society, nothing to their parents, spouses,
children. They were not even much inclined to rationalize their
actions in terms of artistic or literary creativity. They simply
did not like to work, and did so only under coercion of hunger or
cold.

I mention the VER phenomenon because it throws into clear focus
some of the issues which get blurred when we talk about retirement
at 60 versus 70. It is a part of our cultural beliefs that a worker
merits a period of leisure and relaxation late in life. But many
Americans, tend to bristle at the thought of workers who retire at
35 and expect their food, clothing, shelter and other survival needs
to be met by the efforts of others. To quote one of the men
interviewed by Lefkowitz: "Remember it's guys like you who work who
let guys like me not work. You finance me. If enough of you lived
like me, it'd make my life a lot more difficult" (p. 359).

I suspect that most of you will respond to this by saying, cut
him off of welfare, make him work if he wants to eat. But then we
get into the question: At what age do we switch from the benign
view of retirement to a hostile view of the nonworker as a parasite
living off the productive efforts of the working population? And to
what extent is there a danger that the working individual will rebel
against this kind of exploitation, with consequences which could be
disastrous not only for the VER parasites but also for the
legitimate retirees?

Commitment to the work ethic. Andrisani refers to the problem
of youth unemployment as weakening the attachment of individuals to
what we call the "work ethic", the notion that each has an
obligation to help produce the goods and services which we consume.
This attachment is being weakened not only among poor blacks and
other minorities, but among middle-class youth as well. Sarason
(1977) discusses cases of young people who skip from job to job,
sampling many kinds of activities, but essentially living off their
parents and refusing to make a work commitment. Sarason writes
approvingly of this, saying that choice of a lifetime career
requires more than casual consideration. However, it seems possible
that those who postpone a career choice for years will never
establish such a commitment.

To the extent that employers may be concerned about developing a
stable work force for the future, they might well be considering
changes such as seeing to it that young employees entering the work
force have some success experiences, and meet a friendly reception.
One suggestion has been that an older worker be asked to take on

each newcomer as a protege or buddy to be helped in learning the
ropes and conforming to expectations. This might also be beneficial
to the ego of the older employee.

The illiterate younger group. Discussions of the younger worker
problem have laid emphasis on the young, bright, well-educated
worker who resents fragmented repetitive work assignments. But,
regrettably, American industry is also faced with a segment of the
younger work force which is functionally illiterate; many of them do
not speak English well, and even larger numbers do not read
instructions accurately. Evidence is inconclusive as to whether
this group is expanding or shrinking, but it is much too large to be
ignored. Thus planners must consider the retention of some
simplified, repetitive jobs simply in order to provide openings for
applicants who could not handle the enriched assignments now being
established.

Demands for leisure time. Even among the brighter and
well-educated workers there is a demand for more leisure time.
Zimpel (1974) described interviews with some young steelworkers, in
which one young man was asked why he worked only four days a week.
His reply was: "Because I can't quite make it on three days a week."
Thirty years ago value-systems emphasized material possessions;
today a substantial amount of leisure time seems to be viewed as
more important. But absenteeism is expensive for the employer; and,
as noted above, such loss of production tends to increase the
"dependency burden" on those who are on the job. Obviously we need
more research on causes and cures of absenteeism, and as well we can
use information on keeping older workers in production for a longer
work-life.

Employer tactics. I think that, in addition to concern with
government policies as these affect a changing work force, we should
give at least brief attention to what employers are doing. Problems
of dissatisfaction among young workers, absenteeism, frequent
turnover, use of drugs and alcohol on the job, etc., are recognized
at all levels of American industry. While not enough is being done,
in my opinion, there are signs of concern with trying to increase
work commitment and to win worker cooperation in the enterprise.

Job redesign has been a popular phrase among industrial
psychologists in recent years. This may take many forms: job
enlargement, which usually means that a worker does one repetitious
job for a few hours, then is shifted to another. It is hypothesized
that this will relieve boredom, but the results have not been every
encouraging. A second type of job enrichment, which means giving
the worker a less-fragmented task with more room to make some
decisions on his own; e.g., instead of screwing on a single valve,
the worker might assemble a carburetor by himself and test it for
quality. Most workers seem to respond favorably to job enrichment,

although there are some who prefer the simplified repetitive
arrangement. The latter group includes more older employees but
some younger individuals also react in this way. Ideally, jobs
would be tailor-made for each individual, but since the volume of
production required by our population prohibits this, the employer
would probably be wise to enrich some jobs and keep some simple,
permitting transfers to some extent to allow for self-selection, and
presumably thus elevate satisfaction and commitment.

Quality of Work Life. Another popular phrase of this decade is
"Quality of Work Life" or QWL. Much of the QWL effort involves job
enrichment but the phrase includes the development of employee
groups (such as "quality control circles", in which workers discuss
ways to improve quality of the product) and meetings of committees
of workers with a group from management.

There can be little doubt that giving workers a feeling that
they have a voice in decisions affecting them will increase
satisfaction and reduce turnover. It is not clear that workers will
continue to perceive these job redesign measures as genuine
participation if management consistently overrules worker proposals,
or if financial stringencies force layoff of workers who have been
sincerely cooperative.

The QWL movement has been defended on the ground that "job
satisfaction and life satisfaction are closely intertwined." The
evidence does not support this; Meltzer and Stagner (1980) found
that while job satisfaction increased with age, life satisfaction
declined. Life satisfaction may be affected by family and community
problems which are hardly likely to change simply because the work
environment has changed.

There is another reason why I am skeptical about employer
efforts to improve workers' satisfaction. Such efforts readily
degenerate into paternalism. Company-provided nurseries, housing,
stores, and so on, often become points of conflict, not bases for
friendly feelings. American unions have campaigned on the slogan,
"Pay us good wages and we will take care of our outside activities
to suit ourselves." I think the American need for autonomy will
work against QWL programs aimed at affecting satisfaction off the
job.

Small work groups. A form of job redesign advocated by many QWL
consultants is the shift from the assembly line to a series of small
work groups, each responsible for a subassembly or some component
which can be viewed as a finished product, although it will
ultimately be part of a larger product. The Saab and Volvo plants
in Sweden are cited as good examples of the success of this job
arrangement (Frank and Hackman, 1975).

It is noteworthy that six UAW members who went to Sweden to try this small-group design did not approve of it; they liked the line better. The reasons for this are not clear and probably merit further study. However, one point which followers of Kurt Lewin tend to gloss over is what Irving Janis has called the "tyranny of the small group." He refers to the fact that groups can be quite cruel in isolating or ejecting a nonconformist member. Instances of such behavior will be found in several of the case studies of redesigned operations.

My reason for bringing up this particular point is to note that we know very little about intergenerational conflict in small groups. If an older employee is in a group with five young people, he/she may find it difficult to function and may become quite unhappy. The reverse, of course, is also possible. We need to know more about this aspect of age differences in the work context.

Organizational development. There is also a widespread attempt to improve or modify organizational structures in the hope that they will become both more efficient and more satisfying to the managerial employees who are primarily affected. Most experts encourage firms to move from System I toward System IV (Likert) or from Type A to Type B (Argyris). Each implies a change to a flatter organizational structure with a reduction in person-to-person supervision, as in the case of job enrichment at the shop-floor level. Some of these experiments seem to have improved satisfaction and efficiency; others have been abandoned in favor of a return to a more authoritarian pattern.

This is relevant to the question of aging in that the traditional tall or pyramidal structure had very few openings at the top. Thus the beginning manager may have perceived little chance of reaching a high-level post. At the same time, there was a pyramidal age structure (older employees died off or left) so there were fewer competitors for these top jobs. Today, with more employees remaining healthy into their later years, the situation would be more frustrating. Thus, it can be argued that a flat structure, with many middle-level managerial posts and very few at the top, will be more satisfying in that more managers will reach an almost-top position and experience relative success. However, intensely ambitious, competitive individuals will not like such a structure; they will probably leave and establish their own firms.

Intergenerational conflict among employees. The preceding paragraph points to conflict between younger and older managers competing for promotions. But there are similar conflicts in rank-and-file groups.

Union officials are particularly aware of conflicts over contract settlements. Younger members tend to emphasize immediate

wage gains; they want money for better housing, recreational
facilities, and family needs. Older members are more interested in
pension benefits, better insurance programs, and the like.
Controversies over such issues have been bitter in some unions.

Layoff policy is also a source of conflict. The usual union
response to an employer request for lower wage costs is to vote for
layoffs as opposed to cutting hourly rates. This penalizes the
younger members while protecting the older group. Substantial
hostility directed toward union officers has been a consequence of
this. The tradition within unions of favoring seniority was of
course founded on the need to prevent favoritism on the part of the
supervisors, but since officers of the local are usually older
workers, they are beneficiaries of this policy and are resented as a
result.

It is somewhat heartening to find, in a Harris Poll, that most
Americans, including the young, oppose reduction of social security
benefits. But this does not involve any cash outlay by the young
respondents. In union debates the conflict becomes considerably
more apparent.

Do younger workers urge the oldster to retire? The evidence is
ambiguous. In 1977, when Social Security bankruptcy was threatened,
I asked several hundred UAW retirees "Did you feel any pressure from
other employees to retire?" Of those responding, 61 said "yes;" 397
said "no" (Stagner, 1979). But to another question, "Did you think
it was time for you to get out and make room for a younger person?"
the answers were quite different. 384 said "yes;" only 85 said
"no." We cannot say that the "yes" replies indicated a subtle
sensitivity to resentment by the young, but the possibility is
obvious.

Keeping older workers in the labor force. The statistics are
clear; most workers and managers prefer to retire at age 60 or
perhaps a little earlier. This adversely affects the "dependency
ratio" in that we have fewer producers with no decrease in
consumers. It is thus not surprising that managers have
experimented with ways to keep some of these retirees partially
productive. One method is the adoption of limited work schedules,
often called flextime; another is the farming out of work, allowing
the employee to work at home. Each, of course, can apply to others
than retirees or near-retirees, but since our interest is in the
aging problem, I shall treat them in that context.

Flextime allows the older worker to reduce working hours without
complete separation from the job. In some firms two older employees
split one job, each working 20 hours per week. Workers may be
allowed to come in mornings (or afternoons), or on alternate days.
This type of arrangement is most efficient when the job does not

involve downtime of expensive equipment or a shutting-off of important service to customers when the employee is off duty. Experience with flextime seem to be mixed and no consensus has developed with regard to its utility for keeping some productive benefits by utilizing older workers part-time.

The process of permitting employees to work away from a central location is also active today. One type, a revival of the "cottage industries" of 200 years ago, is vigorously opposed by union officials because hourly wage rates, safety hazards, and other matters of concern to the union, cannot be monitored if work is done in the employee's home. From the viewpoint of the older workers there are obvious advantages: quiet, an end to fighting traffic, a chance to take a break without disrupting an assembly line, and so on.

One particular version of this movement seems less likely to evoke less antagonism from unions. This involves placing a computer terminal in the employee's home, so that work of an information-processing character can go on exactly as it would have at the office. Little or no supervision is needed, and job performance can be audited as well as if the individual were physically on the premises. Judicious applications of this and other innovations may help us to reduce the "dependency ratio" and maintain the economy with less inflation.

If these arrangements are designed to be integrated with a retirement program, some modifications of Social Security regulations may be necessary. Instead of postponing early retirement, as the current administration proposes, it may be preferable to allow some earnings during the period of "early" retirement without penalty. The economic gains might more than compensate for any costs to the system. Alternatively, companies may permit earlier payments from pension accounts, supplemented by part-time earnings as suggested above.

It may also be possible to induce some fully-retired persons to re-enter productive roles. Gray and Morse (1980) found that, of about 1000 middle-level managers, 40% took up some part-time (or full-time) employment after retirement. This is in sharp contrast with the UAW retirees (Stagner, 1979) of whom less than 20% show any interest in obtaining paid jobs. Managerial retirees would, of course, have access to more openings as consultants and to physically easy jobs; they may also have suffered a sharper drop in income and thus felt more pressure to resume work after retiring. There can be little doubt that, when the percentage of workers over 60 does increase greatly, it will be necessary for more of them to remain productively employed or inflation will rise and standards of living will fall.

It will perhaps be noted that in the foregoing remarks I have
moved back and forth from concern with management, to concern with
workers, to concern with unions and union leaders. Perhaps we
should also include a concern with consumers. Decisions about
employment policy and about retirement programs are going to affect
all of the groups I have mentioned. It would, I think, be most
unfortunate if we focused exclusively on the interests of elderly
workers, or of young workers, or of managers, or of union leaders,
without considering the impact of policies on the production of good
and services for the consuming public. All of these interest groups
compete for our attention and our support. The aging employee, and
the retiree, continue to be consumers. It is to their interest --
as well as to younger individuals -- that the supply of goods and
services remain adequate for our desired standard of living. It is
for this reason that governmental and private employer policies must
seek optimal use of employee talents at all age levels.

Summary

The changing age composition of the work force must be
subdivided into a set of different problems before research
recommendations can be offered. In the immediate future we may
expect to see a slight decline in younger applicants for work, a
substantial increase in the "prime age" cohort, and a very slight
increase in the older contingent. However, trends toward early
retirement continue, meaning that no immediate problem of recruiting
older employees to stay on the job, or of redesigning jobs to
accommodate them, is cause for concern.

I think the panel sees a need for more research on the
entry-level younger worker, with two sharply different groups in
mind. (1) We need to know more about how to develop "work
commitment" in young people, especially the bright, well-educated
individuals who are unhappy with assembly-line jobs. (2) We also
must devise job assignments and supervisory procedures for drawing
into productive jobs the thousands of functional illiterates --
immigrants and others -- who otherwise become part of the
"dependency burden."

For the prime-age cohort, current efforts at job enrichment,
organizational development and participation in decisions seem
well-conceived to reduce dissatisfaction, mid-career change, and so
on. However, there is a substantial need for research on why some
well-trained professionals and technicians quit for lower level jobs
of less value to society; and within both blue-collar and
white-collar populations we need more information on who will
respond favorably -- or unfavorably -- to proposed changes in work
design.

For older workers we need much more precisely focused research on differential decline of varying abilities, and test batteries which will spotlight relative strong points so that the older worker who is willing to stay on can be utilized optimally. Profiles of job demands and worker abilities can be matched, and evidence indicates that when workers are thus placed, job satisfaction increases, with a probable increase in productivity and work output. We also need more research on the factors causing older workers to opt for early retirement, and on devices which might be persuasive in keeping workers on the job. The broad issues of inflation and the "dependency ratio" cannot be separated from the microeconomic variables of work commitment, job satisfaction, job layouts, and assignments, and early retirement.

Various groups are concerned with and must cooperate on such research programs. Obviously the workers themselves, older and younger, have important interests at stake and must be widely consulted. A research program which appears to be aimed solely at more effective exploitation of workers, whether young or old, will be a failure.

Managers must also be involved in research planning, because the breakdown of some stereotyped beliefs about older workers may prove to be crucial to policy changes. If managers are not drawn into planning and execution of research, they will continue to ignore research data in setting up personnel policies.

Union officers must have a voice in the planning and development of research on the effects of aging. Unions represent the major institutional tool available to workers for defending their interests and for demanding a voice in operating decisions within industry and government. Unions also have increasing problems which revolve around the changing age composition of the American labor force.

Finally, the consumer -- or the population at large -- has a stake, if not an active interest, in the results of research and modification of work environments. Dependent members of the population -- those who consume but do not produce -- may be perceived as burdens. We do not expect young children to be productive, but the absentees, the very-early retirees, the mid-career dropouts, and the normal retired group are potentially of concern to policy-makers. If the Conference leads to research ventures which will help us optimize the functioning of the American economic system, it will have been truly worth while.

References

Baugher, D. Is the older worker inherently incompetent? Aging and Work, 1978, 1, 243-250.

Belbin, R. M. _Training methods for older workers_. Paris: OECD,
     1965.

Caplan, R. D., Cobb, S., French, J. R. P. Jr., Harrison, R. V., and
     Pinneau, S. R. Jr. _Job demands and worker health_. Washington,
     D.C.: HEW Publication (NIOSH) 75-160, 1975.

Clopton, W. Personality and career change. _Industrial Gerontology_,
     1973 (No. 17), 9-17.

Craft, J. A., Doctors, S. I., Shkop, Y. M., and Benecki, T. J.
     Simulated management perceptions, hiring decisions, and age.
     Aging and Work, 1979, _2_, 95-102.

Dubin, S. S. (Ed.) _Professional obsolescence_. Lexington, Mass.:
     D. C. Heath, 1972.

Frank, L. L., and Hackman, R. J. A failure of job enrichment: the
     case of the change that wasn't. _Journal of Applied Behavioral
     Science_, 1975, _11_, 413-436.

Fritz, D. Decision makers and the changing retirement scene. _Aging
     and Work_, 1978, _1_, 221-230.

Goldstein, I. L. Training in work organizations. _Annual Review of
     Psychology_, 1980, _31_, 229-272.

Gray, S., and Morse, D. Retirement and re-engagement: changing
     work options for older workers. _Aging and Work_, 1980, _3_,
     103-112.

Horn, J. L., and Cattell, R. B. Age differences in fluid and
     crystallized intelligence. _Acta Psychologica_, 1967, _26_,
     107-129.

Lefkowitz, B. _Breaktime: living without work in a nine-to-five
     world_. New York: Penguin, 1979.

Lifson, K. A. Errors in time-study judgments of industrial work
     pace. _Psychological Monographs_, 1953, _67_, No. 355.

McFarland, R. A. The need for functional age measurements in
     industrial gerontology. _Industrial Gerontology_, 1973, No. 19.

Meier, E. L., and Kerr, E. A. Capabilities of middle-aged and older
     workers. _Industrial Gerontology_, 1976, _3_, 147-156.

Meltzer, H., and Stagner, R. Social psychology of aging in
     industry. _Professional Psychology_, 1980, _11_, 436-444.

Muchinsky, P. M. Age and job facet satisfaction: a conceptual
     reconsideration. _Aging and Work_, 1978, _1_, 175-180.

Mullick, B. _The effects of age of the perceiver, locus of control,
     locus of causality, and responsibility on attitudes toward the
     elderly_. Unpublished Ph.D. dissertation, Wayne State
     University, 1981.

Owens, W. A. Jr. Age and mental abilities: a second adult
     follow-up. _Journal of Educational Psychology_, 1966, _57_,
     311-325.

Phillips, J. S., Barrett, G. V., and Rush, M. C. Job structure and
     work satisfaction. _Aging and Work_, 1978, _1_, 109-119.

Price, R. L., Thompson, P. H., and Dalton, G. W. A longitudinal
     study of technological obsolescence. _Research Management_, 1975
     (November), 22-28.

Pursell, E. D., Dossett, D. L., and Latham, G. P. Obtaining valid predictors by minimizing rating errors in the criterion. Personnel Psychology, 1980, 33, 91-96.

Quinn, R. P., and Shepard, L. J. The 1972-73 quality of employment survey. Ann Arbor, Mich.: Institute for Social Research, University of Michigan, 1974.

Rosen, B., and Jerdee, T. H. Influence of age stereotypes on managerial decisions. Journal of Applied Psychology, 1976, 61, 428-432.

Rosen, B., Jerdee, T. H., and Lunn, R. O. Retirement policies and management decision. Aging and Work, 1980, 3, 239-246.

Saleh, S. D., and Otis, J. L. Sources of job satisfaction and their effects on attitudes toward retirement. Journal of Industrial Psychology, 1963, 1, 101-106.

Sarason, S. B. Work, aging, and social change. New York: The Free Press, 1977.

Sheppard, H. L. Towards an industrial gerontology. New York: National Council on the Aging, 1970.

Sheppard, H. L., and Herrick, N. Q. Where have all the robots gone? New York: The Free Press, 1972.

Sheppard, H. L., and Rix, S. E. The graying of working America: the coming crisis of retirement age policy. New York: The Free Press, 1977.

Stagner, R. Boredom on the assembly line: age and personality variables. Industrial Gerontology, 1975, 2, 23-44.

Stagner, R. Propensity to work: an important variable in retiree behavior. Aging and Work, 1979, 2, 161-172.

Zimpel, L. Man against work. Grand Rapids, Mich.: W. B. Eerdmans Co., 1974.

PART II

THE 1990 GENDER MIX

IMPLICATIONS OF THE INCREASING PARTICIPATION OF WOMEN

IN THE WORK FORCE IN THE 1990's

Mary L. Tenopyr

American Telephone and Telegraph Company

Morristown, NJ

All projections are for an increase in women in the work force
by 1990. Although various projections differ, it is likely that 60%
of women of working age will be in the work force in the 1990's.
The implications of this change in women's participation in the
world of work are difficult to determine. However, it can be
assumed that there will be major changes in work by 1990 and that
some of these changes will be effected through the participation of
women in increasing numbers in the work force. Many factors inter-
act in my predictions about what the world of work will be like in
1990.

Energy Costs

One of the factors, which is dominant and will affect the employment of women, is the increasing energy costs. Despite the fact
that feminists have advocated part-time schedules and flex time to
accommodate the working mother with household responsibilities, it
appears that by 1990 energy will result in more fixed hours. Because of the high cost of gasoline, the nine-to-five day will become
common. Also, there will be more dependence on public transportation and on carpools, which do not operate at flexible hours. I
predict also that energy costs will force movement of families back
into the inner cities. The suburban work location, upon which a
large number of automobiles with one driver and no passengers des-
cend, will be rapidly fading out by 1990. As will the suburban
workplace decline in importance, so will typical suburban living,
and women may have more time than they had previously because they
do not have large yards to take care of and are not serving as
chauffeurs to take children to schools, to basketball games, and
other events. Another feature of the 1990's may be small satellite

69

locations, located near small cities where workers can be accommodated with minimal energy costs. It appears that energy costs will
have then tendencies which affect the employment of women in various
ways. Some of these are counterbalancing. For example, although
there may be movement away from areas requiring an automobile for
transportation, there may be movement toward spacious geographical
areas where home heating is not a big cost. I also predict that
there will be a marked decrease in business travel and in travel-
related industries such as motels, hotels, airlines, automobile
production.

Technology Change

At the same time, there will be an increase in the use of electronic communications. Thus, there will be a change in opportunities for employment of women. The advancing technology, particularly in the computer communications field, will have a marked effect
on the employment of women. What I see the computer doing is increasing the standard deviation of job difficulty. As the computer
invades even the smallest of work operations, it is clear that there
are going to be a large number of low level jobs of the data entry
type. The skilled clerical jobs will be fewer in number and, at the
other extreme, there will be a need for programmers, systems
analysts and maintenance technicians to keep the computer running.
The same thing is happening to a lesser extent to craft work. As
numerically controlled equipment, such as the computer-operated
milling machines, becomes more common, the skilled machinist will be
replaced by a combination of data entry personnel and programmers.
The communications field is one I see booming over the next decade.
There is a fine line between voice transmission by the typical telephone and data transmission. There will be a need for scientists to
develop the new technology needed in an era in which communications
of necessity must be more and more by electronic means. People in
the hard sciences will be particularly in demand. Electronics engineers, computer science specialists and others in related disciplines will be very much needed. The hard sciences unfortunately
are one area in which women have not made substantial inroads.

At the same time, as we will need more hard scientists, we will
have a greater need for technically trained managers. Although my
colleagues in industrial and organizational psychology for the most
part are concerned with the selection and development of the generalist manager, I believe that the technically trained manager will
be the manager needed in the future. There is just too much technical complication to business today and in the future to be handled
by generalist managers. Advancing technology also interacts with
the employment of women in another way. With advancing technology
there will probably be increasing life spans and a potentially
longer work life for women who already have a potentially longer
work life than men. Although as women progress in the type of work
men used to do exclusively, their life spans may decrease.

Economic Pressures

The general economic situation we are facing now will also be a factor in the employment of women. I believe that inflation over the next decade will not really come under complete control, mainly because of rising energy costs, coupled with the inflation psychology. The days of 2% or 3% inflation per year, I think, are long past us. We will probably consider it excellent government management if annual inflation is as much as 8% or so. Thus, with ever increasing costs, women will simply have to work in order to have some income to furnish the basic necessities of life. I believe that although taxes will not rise perhaps as much as they have in the past, wealth redistribution will continue despite relatively conservative policies of government. With wealth redistribution, taxes on the working person's income will continue to erode the purchasing power of that income and, thus, women again will have to work. Family dissolution, already at a high rate, will undoubtedly continue in the future. Again, women will have to work. Productivity should be a major concern in the future. Unless productivity is raised by a tax cut to spur investment in R&D and by other government actions, there is going to be less of the economic pie for each of us to share. Thus again, women will have to work. And social Security taxes, because of the cost of the program, may be markedly increased relative to benefits. Sophisticated younger people now in the work force are starting to realize that they may never live to collect Social Security. Thus, providing security for old age provides another reason for women to work. Also, if Social Security benefits are decreased markedly, working life of women may be increased simply because one cannot afford to retire without the cushion of a well-funded Social Security Benefit Program.

There has been much discussion about the possibility of redesigning the workplace to accommodate the physical capacities of women. Such redesign of equipment and tools would indeed facilitate the placement of women in the well paying, physically demanding job which are now held primarily by men. I suggest that the basic economic problems, which will probably continue to face us, will prevent major redesigns of tools and equipment to accommodate women. Thus, I do not see a large future for women in the heavily physical work. As has been pointed out in the Wall Street Journal (1980), for a number of years employers have been substituting labor for capital; and as long as the supply of strong men to fill physically demanding jobs is available, it is unlikely, given the present economic climate, that jobs will be redesigned to accommodate women. Thus, energy costs and related economic conditions will undoubtedly lead to more women in the work force. It is difficult to predict what is going to happen in the economic sphere, but it appears at the present time that all of the conditions are right to force women into the work force and require them to have longer working careers than they otherwise might have had. Also, economics combined with

the technological advances may change the type of work which is
available to everyone, not just women.

Social Policy

The social conditions which will prevail a decade or more from
now are almost as difficult to predict as economic conditions. It
is clear, I believe, that women and minorities will continue to ask
to share more in the economic benefits of society. Despite an
apparent trend towards conservatism in the country, I do not foresee
a marked lessening of affirmative action efforts. I believe that
the administration and the courts will continue to support strong
equal employment opportunity policies. One of the factors which
determines the social policy of the government is obviously economics. Massive affirmative action efforts were possible in the late
1960's when there was almost full employment. As long as there was
almost full employment, there was little conflict regarding the
merits of affirmative action. However, if the economic pie continues to get smaller, there may be some marked conflicts relative to
affirmative action. Previous federal administrations have not
really faced the question which is predominant in this area, i.e.,
whether there should be equality of opportunity or equality of outcome. Those who argue for equality of outcome and those who argue
for equality of opportunity possibly are not greatly different in
their philosophy as some might believe. Equality of outcome involves a certain amount of wealth redistribution on the basis of the
awarding of jobs. It is clear that equality of opportunity based on
traditional notions of merit will result in the exclusion, on a
group basis, of large numbers from the job market. These people
will have to be supported by transfer payments of some sort. Thus,
the dilemma is how best to provide for the support of our whole population, and the question is whether redistribution should take
place by the vehicle of job allocation or of welfare and other
social payments.

The testing issue, which has long been before the courts, and
the subject of government pronouncements is really nothing except a
pawn in this controversy which has not been articulated too well by
the government. I really doubt whether future administrations will
face this problem squarely and we will probably continue to have
many legal proceedings regarding the way employers select their employees.

In a related social area, I believe that there will continue to
be conflicts among women regarding questions like the passage of
ERA. This type of conflict will tend to reduce the amount of
political influence women will have regarding employment opportunities in the future. However, as more and more women must work out
of necessity, I suspect conflict among the women's groups will be
lessened. I believe that women will have a long, hard struggle to

be accepted in many high level jobs. The years since the passage of
the Civil Rights Act of 1964 have really not changed things that
much regarding the status of women in executive and other policy-
making positions. Women in the Baby Boom Era are now reaching the
age at which they are competing for the policy-making positions. As
the competition is difficult, even for men, I think women will perhaps experience many career frustrations on an individual basis and
tend to become more militant. Job satisfaction in the 1990's will
become as much of a problem for the middle-aged, both men and women,
as it is now with the younger entrants into the work force.

Education

Events in the educational system, too, will have an effect on
the future makeup of the work force and, particularly, the employment of women. We are all aware of the Scholastic Aptitude Test
decline (College Entrance Examination Board, 1977) and the need for
better public secondary school education. I predict that there will
be more of an effort than even now is being put forth to provide for
accountability of the educational system. Competency testing has
been brought forth by 36 states and many local school districts are
introducing competency testing to help provide for accountability of
the schools. One problem that women in particular face is the
status of higher education institutions today. As the baby boom
generation has passed through the higher education system, these institutions are often having financial difficulties and are recruiting students to make up for declining revenues. There are rumors to
the effect that educational standards are being compromised in order
to keep students in the system. Such activities can cause new
social problems for both men and women. If the college degree, the
traditional key to the better life, is compromised, there may be
many dashed hopes among those entering the work force a decade from
now.

Defense Requirements

Another characteristic which will impact the employment of women
in the 1990's is international events. Again, predictions in this
area are difficult to make. However, I believe it is clear that international tensions will probably remain at such a level that conscription into the Armed Forces will be necessary. This will remove
younger men from the work force and, thereby, open up for some time
entry level jobs for women. At the same time, however, conscription
will create a large supply of men with veterans preference for public jobs in the Federal Government and many state and local govern-
ments; thus, closing off a number of better jobs for women.

Problem Summation

The conditions, then, I see prevailing in the 1990's are these.
I see large numbers of women entering the work force. I believe

that current projections of the number of women in the work force
may be low. There is a large combination of circumstances forcing
women to work: inflation, increased taxes, need for old age security and family instability. Furthermore, I see women as having
great difficulties in the workplace of the 1990's unless there are
research and research-based interventions. I see large numbers of
women in very simple data entry-type jobs, with few economic and
social rewards. I think we will experience high turnover in these
jobs and be faced with a largely dissatisfied group of people. Unless our education system and social system changes through meaningful intervention, I see few women able to compete for the increasing
number of jobs in the hard sciences and technical management. I see
relatively few women in the physically demanding jobs. I really do
not expect to see many more women in jobs like construction worker
than we have right now. I do see new opportunities in retail and
service where part-time jobs may become available when stores and
service organizations adopt new hours to accommodate the needs of
women who are working rigidly scheduled nine-to-five jobs. Thus, I
see women as a progressively disenchanted group in the 1990's. Economic pressures, as opposed to opportunities, will be a real problem
for many women. Boring, tedious jobs in which one is communicating
with the computer will become even more commonplace than they are
now, leading to great strains. Current patterns of leisure activities, which many people enjoy now, will be curtailed as people move
into the crowded, inner city and are unable to jump into a large,
family car and travel long distances for interesting vacations,
shopping trips, etc. Child care will be a problem. The problem of
fewer opportunities for better jobs will add to the stress. The
unstable, personal lives, as a result of our tendency to have less
impact from the family, will add also to the stress. I see the
effects of all this stress as varying. I suspect the women's movement will become more vocal. I think you will see women moving more
toward the trade unions in order to achieve their aims. Others may
drop out, and we may see increased health problems on the part of
some women, and various types of substance abuse.

Research and Educational Needs

What can be done to facilitate a transition into the work life
of a decade from now? First, we need to increase productivity. The
government should provide sensible tax policies so that there can be
investment in research and development which will lead to increased
productivity. In our area of concern, we must mount multi-discipli-
nary efforts in productivity research, and we should, significantly,
include the industrial and organizational psychologist in these
efforts. We must be able to assess the effect of social change on
productivity. We should not only work at the macro level of the
economist and government policies, we should work on individual
workers and groups of workers. In the area of organizational psychology, we need to incorporate sex-related variables and other

realities into our teaching of organizational psychology for both men and women. I have been consistently surprised at how weak our training in organizational psychology is. I am also surprised at how much is wasted on various types of training in business. One example I often think of is the so-called "personal growth training." I am disappointed that our research is not based on harder variables than it is. I would hope that we would develop a base of solid research in industrial and organizational psychology which can be used as a basis for teaching and planning interventions in organizations. We also should become more cognizant of the need for evaluation research. We must evaluate our teaching. We must evaluate our interventions in organization.

I feel we need to pay particular attention to the education of women in technological fields. For example, we should lift age restrictions on scholarships and fellowships. We should develop flexible schedules of classes so that one can pursue a degree at night or on Saturdays. I believe that it is ironic that one can take Contract Bridge at night, but not Calculus. We must work toward upgrading the inner city schools at the possible expense of residential universities in the country which are not accessible to the typical, working woman. We must somehow attack the problem of providing role models in professorial positions. At present, in many of the hard sciences, the tenure track system is essentially clogged up with men. Again, we must evaluate every step. The proper education of women has economic benefits. We need to ensure that not only women, but all people concerned are qualified to assume the high level, organizational roles that will need to be filled in the 1990's. It is clear that education can be the base for starting a beneficent cycle. Increased appropriate education can lead to increased performance which leads to increased productivity which leads, again, to more opportunities where education can be used. We need to study more about the basic abilities of women in technological fields. I am uncomfortable about the stance of Benbow and Stanley (1980) who suggest that women are genetically inferior in mathematical and spatial abilities. However, I welcome their views, because I feel that they will result in considerable research on the abilities of women and eventually help women to develop these abilities in the technological areas where they are most needed.

I also feel we need to provide evaluated, developmental experiences for women in managerial roles. If women are to fill policy-making positions in the future, they must have special attention which is not normally given to men. One can never assume that a man and a woman in the same job have gained the same experience. I am particularly cognizant in my association with younger women, working their way up in organizations, of how little they understand power processes and office interrelations. I do not think our present education programs really teach people how to live in organizations.

I do not know of any way to really impress upon people the way
organizations actually work, as opposed to how they are supposed to
work according to the textbook, without providing them with controlled experience.

Finally, I believe we need to do research now relative to the
possible lifestyles of the 1990's. Working at home, satellite
offices, the new, inner city, all provide avenues for research which
can affect the utilization and satisfaction of women in the work
force in the 1990's. Unless we provide a total integrated research
base, we cannot expect to impact the world of work in the 1990's,
and ensure that it is a productive world which ensures equal opportunity to all Americans.

References

Benbow, C. P. & Stanley, J. C. Sex differences in mathematical
    ability: Fact or artifact? Science, 1980, 210, 1262-1264.
College Entrance Examination Board. On Further Examination: Report
    of the Advisory Panel on the Scholastic Aptitude Test Decline.
    New York: College Entrance Examination Board, 1977.
Trouble at work -- Joblessness may soar because of changes in
    economy since 1975. Wall Street Journal, July 1, 1980, 1, 11.

THE FEMINIZATION OF THE LABOR FORCE: RESEARCH FOR

INDUSTRIAL/ORGANIZATIONAL PSYCHOLOGY

Veronica F. Nieva

The Urban Institute

Washington, D. C.

Women Workers in the 1990s

Projections of the female labor force to the 1990's (Smith, 1979) present a picture not radically different from the labor force today. The female labor force has grown rapidly in this century, especially since World War II. In 1978, there were over 40 million women in the labor force; about half of all women age 16 and over. By 1990, 52 million are expected to be in the labor force; about 55% of the women over 16. Other estimates were made by another study (Flaim & Fullerton, 1978) which had three different scenarios depending on varying assumptions about future growth in the U.S. work force. Under their low growth assumption, their labor force estimates projected close to 51 million women (a 54% participation rate); their intermediate growth assumption projected about 54 million (a 57% participation rate), and their high growth assumption projected about 57 million women (a 60% participation rate) in 1990. Under any of these circumstances, therefore, more than half of the women would be in the labor force, and they would constitute close to half of the entire labor force.

Nearly all the increase is expected in women aged 25 to 50, from a combination of an increase in their absolute numbers (by about 12 million) and an increase in their labor force participation rates from about 55% in 1975 to about 63%. Most of the increase will be among married women with minor children.

Another large segment of the female labor force will consist, then as now, of divorced and separated women. Continuing a longterm

trend, statistics show that in 1977 more than 73% of divorced women
and 55% of separated women were working; on the average, divorced
and separated women are more likely to be in the labor force than
married women with husband present. Divorced and separated women
accounted for 13% of the female work force and were responsible for
more than one-quarter of the unusually large labor force expansion
since 1975 (Grossman, 1978).

There may be even more women in the 1990 labor force than these
projections show if certain things happen -- e.g., if the gap
between male and female wages narrows, if attitudes about the
appropriate roles for men and women continue to change, and if more
job opportunities open up for women. Table 1 and 2 show projections
of the female labor force in 1990 (taken from Smith, 1979; Flaim and
Fullerton, 1978). If present trends continue, women in the 1990's
will be working for longer continuous periods of time, although intermittent attachment to the labor force will still characterize the
work lives of women more than men, because of greater turnover associated with their low-paid jobs and interruptions due to child-
rearing demands. At present, both women and employers tend to
underestimate the length of time that the women will be in the labor
force (Barrett, 1979).

It is clear that more women will be looking for jobs in the
1990s. Where will they find them? What are the chances that
women's status relative to men in the labor force will improve from
the status quo? Statistics show that past increases in female labor
force participation has not been accompanied by greater parity
between working men and women. Women still earn much less than men,
have higher unemployment rates, occupy dead-end jobs, and are in
crowded women's occupations that have lower status and lower pay
than men's occupations. In fact, female employment in crowded female occupations such as the clerical field and service occupations
rose as a percentage of total female employment from the 1960's to
the 1970's (U.S. Department of Labor, 1978). Women have not made
much progress in occupying high level positions of authority, even
in female-dominated occupations. This less than optimistic picture
becomes even bleaker when one considers the influence of a weakened
economy, which generally lowers the demand for all workers.

Needed Research

Social science research must respond to these two major aspects
of the present and future workforce--the demographic makeup of the
women in the workforce, and the persisting inequity between men and
women in the labor force. Although some questions implied by each
of these features of the workforce would clearly overlap, let us for
the moment examine them separately in terms of the information needs
of the future.

Table 1. Labor Force Projections for 1990 Based on 1964-77 Trends and 1977 Populations (Smith, 1979).

	Population (thousands)			Labor force (thousands)			Participation rate (percent)		
	Actual 1977 (March)	Pro- jected 1990	Pro- jected change	Actual 1977 (March)	Pro- jected 1990	Pro- jected change	Actual 1977 (March)	Pro- jected 1990	Pro- jected change
AGE 16-19									
Never-married	7,248	5,790	-1,458	3,421	3,561	140	47.2	61.5	14.3
Married, spouse present	876	700	-176	436	470	34	49.8	67.1	17.3
No children under 18	514	411	-103	311	337	26	60.5	82.1	21.6
Children 6-17 only	5	4	-1	3	2	-1	60.0	60.0	0
Children under 6	357	285	-72	122	131	9	34.2	46.0	11.8
Other ever-married	178	142	-36	89	87	-2	50.0	61.3	11.3
No children under 18	100	80	-20	61	58	-3	60.7	72.6	11.9
Children 6-17 only	--	--	--	--	--	--	--	--	--
Children under 6	78	62	-16	28	29	1	35.9	47.2	11.3
Total, 16-19	8,302	6,632	-1,670	3,946	4,118	172	47.5	62.1	14.6
AGE 20-24									
Never-married	4,438	4,030	-408	3,147	2,801	-346	70.9	69.5	-1.4
Married, spouse present	4,591	4,169	-422	2,747	3,020	273	59.8	72.4	12.6
No children under 18	2,070	1,880	-190	1,677	1,658	-19	81.0	88.2	7.2
Children 6-17 only	58	53	-5	33	36	3	56.9	67.7	10.8
Children under 6	2,463	2,236	-227	1,037	1,326	289	42.1	59.3	17.2
Other ever-married	775	704	-71	484	481	-3	62.4	68.3	5.9
No children under 18	340	309	-31	255	231	-24	75.1	74.6	-0.5
Children 6-17 only	37	34	-3	24	32	8	64.9	95.0	30.1
Children under 6	398	361	-37	205	218	13	51.4	60.3	8.9
Total, 20-24	9,804	8,903	-901	6,378	6,302	-76	65.1	70.8	5.7
Total, 16-24	18,106	15,535	-2,571	10,324	10,420	96	57.0	67.1	10.1

Table 1. (continued)

	Population (thousands)			Labor force (thousands)			Participation rate (percent)		
	Actual 1977 (March)	Pro- jected 1990	Pro- jected change	Actual 1977 (March)	Pro- jected 1990	Pro- jected change	Actual 1977 (March)	Pro- jected 1990	Pro- jected change
AGE 25-34									
Never-married	1,959	2,458	499	1,640	2,043	403	83.7	83.1	-0.6
Married, spouse present	12,102	15,185	3,083	6,317	10,347	4,030	52.2	68.1	15.9
No children under 18	2,139	2,684	545	1,743	2,550	807	81.5	95.0	13.5
Children 6-17 only	3,153	3,956	803	1,904	2,995	1,091	60.4	75.7	15.3
Children under 6	6,810	8,545	1,735	2,670	4,802	2,132	39.2	56.2	17.0
Other ever-married	2,360	2,961	601	1,785	2,399	614	75.6	81.0	5.4
No children under 18	647	812	165	575	771	196	88.9	95.0	6.1
Children 6-17 only	911	1,143	232	732	945	213	80.3	82.7	2.4
Children under 6	802	1,006	204	478	683	205	59.6	67.9	8.3
Total, 25-34	16,421	20,605	4,184	9,742	14,789	5,047	59.3	71.8	12.5
AGE 35-44									
Never-married	599	931	332	438	639	201	73.2	68.6	-4.6
Married, spouse present	9,312	14,480	5,168	5,215	9,994	4,779	56.0	69.0	13.0
No children under 18	1,420	2,208	788	916	1,561	645	64.5	70.7	6.2
Children 6-17 only	6,355	9,882	3,527	3,730	7,224	3,494	58.7	73.1	14.4
Children under 6	1,537	2,390	853	569	1,209	640	37.0	50.6	13.6
Other ever-married	2,006	3,119	1,113	1,457	2,382	925	72.6	76.4	3.8
No children under 18	536	833	297	434	771	337	80.9	92.6	11.7
Children 6-17 only	1,259	1,958	699	914	1,422	508	72.6	72.6	0
Children under 6	211	328	117	109	189	80	51.7	57.7	6.0
Total, 35-44	11,917	18,530	6,613	7,110	13,015	5,905	59.7	70.2	10.5

	Population (thousands)			Labor force (thousands)			Participation rate (percent)		
	Actual 1977 (March)	Pro-jected 1990	Pro-jected change	Actual 1977 (March)	Pro-jected 1990	Pro-jected change	Actual 1977 (March)	Pro-jected 1990	Pro-jected change
AGE 45-54									
Never-married	512	548	36	382	420	38	74.7	76.6	1.9
Married, spouse present	9,214	9,856	642	4,769	5,769	1,000	51.8	58.5	6.7
No children under 18	5,384	5,759	375	2,880	3,455	575	53.5	60.0	6.5
Children 6-17 only	3,706	3,964	258	1,849	2,263	414	49.9	57.1	7.2
Children under 6	124	133	9	40	51	11	32.6	38.0	5.4
Other ever-married	2,322	2,484	162	1,600	1,713	113	68.9	69.0	0.1
No children under 18	1,595	1,706	111	1,148	1,232	84	72.0	72.2	0.2
Children 6-17 only	698	747	49	438	466	28	62.8	62.4	-0.4
Children under 6	29	31	2	14	15	1	48.4	48.4	0
Total, 45-54	12,048	12,888	840	6,751	7,902	1,151	56.0	61.3	5.3
Total, 25-54	40,386	52,023	11,637	23,603	35,706	12,103	58.4	68.6	10.2

Table 2. Civilian Labor Force Participation Rates Based on Three Different Growth Paths to 1990 (Flaim and Fullerton, 1978).

Growth paths	Civilian labor force							Civilian labor force participation rates			
	Actual (millions)		Projected (millions)		Annual percent change			Actual		Projected	
	1970	1977	1985	1990	1970 to 1977	1977 to 1985	1985 to 1990	1970	1977	1985	1990
Total											
High growth path			117.0	125.6		2.3	1.4			67.7	69.7
Intermediate growth path	82.7	97.4	113.0	119.4	2.3	1.9	1.1	60.4	62.3	65.3	66.2
Low growth path			108.9	113.5		1.4	.8			63.0	63.0
Men											
High growth path			65.0	68.2		1.6	1.0			79.4	80.0
Intermediate growth path	51.2	57.4	63.0	65.1	1.7	1.2	.7	79.7	77.7	77.0	76.4
Low growth path			61.2	62.5		.8	.4			74.7	73.3
Women											
High growth path			52.0	57.4		3.3	2.0			57.1	60.4
Intermediate growth path	31.5	40.0	49.9	54.3	3.4	2.8	1.7	43.3	48.4	54.8	57.1
Low growth path			47.7	51.0		2.2	1.3			52.4	53.8

[1] Compounded continuously

The Demographics of the Workforce

A striking feature of the future labor force is the marked increase of labor force participation of "prime age" women (between 25
and 54), virtually all of whom are expected to be married, and a
large proportion of whom will be mothers with children under
eighteen. The reasons behind this increase include economic explanations -- e.g., increased wages available to women in the paid
labor force, with no corresponding increase in the rewards for working within the home, and a tremendous growth in jobs in the service
sector accompanied by some decrease in the importance of physical
strength in many industrial jobs. Further, worsening economic conditions in recent years have created greater need for married
women's income. From psychologists and sociologists come other explanations, in the form of changes in sex-role attitudes on issues
such as the salience of female achievement, the propriety of employment of mothers with young children and general attitudes towards
working. A recent study of sex-role changes between 1964 and 1974
shows that changes have affected most segments of the population
(Mason, Czakar & Arber, 1976).

The demographics of the emerging workforce puts the spotlight on
certain concepts and questions of interest to Industrial/Organiza-
tional psychologists. The questions that have guided much of I/O
research have generally assumed a male worker or a male manager
(e.g., Stewart, 1978; Gutek, Nakamura & Nieva, 1981), although recent interest in working women has stimulated a flurry of research
on stereotyping and sex differences in various organizational processes such as performance evaluation or job satisfaction. There
has also been increasing interest in women managers and professionals (e.g., Hennig & Jardin, 1977; Gordon & Strober, 1975).

Too often, however, the questions that are being asked are still
the same questions as those that were traditionally asked, with
added attention to the sex of the research subjects. For example,
what are the differences between male and female leaders? What are
the differences between the career aspirations of men and women?
This approach is useful and serves as a check to unstated assumptions about the universality of research findings. However, we need
to go beyond the sex differences model to other kinds of inquiries
that are stimulating serious consideration of issues important to
women workers. Inevitably these will also affect the kinds of questions we would ask about the experience of working for both sexes.

Obviously, the number of questions or issues pertinent to the
changing demographics of the workforce are too many for a session
like this, even if we restrict our field of vision to the questions
that might interest us as applied social, industrial or organizational psychologists. Let me then address what I perceive to be the
two most critical neglected areas to which researchers should attend

-- the linkages between work and family systems, and a related
topic, alternate work and career patterns.

Work and family linkages. By and large, issues related to the
linkages between work and family have been ignored by I/O psychologists, who have tended to treat the worker (traditionally assumed to
be male) outside of a context of other life spheres. Although male
workers had families, the family was not considered their primary
domain, and thus the issues of work-family linkages could be sub-
merged. However, the dramatic increase in the number of women
workers (who are assumed to have the primary family responsibility)
makes it essential to examine work-family links. This interest is
given added impetus by what appears to be a trend towards a re-
valuing of private and family life by professionals and younger
people (Bailyn & Schein, 1976; Gartner & Reissman, 1974) of both
sexes.

The relationship between work and family is not entirely new
ground for research. Economists and sociologists have looked into
this general issue in terms of the broad connections between variables such as occupation and divorce rates, fertility and labor
force participation, wife employment status and family well-being
and stability. There remain many unanswered questions, however,
when one goes beyond the behavioral associations found in large
populations, to the interactions of a particular job, occupation and
family structures and processes. This is largely unexplored terri-
tory.

Role concepts provide a useful approach to the study of specific
work-family links. A number of inquiries can be formulated using
role concepts. One set of questions revolves around the issues of
role intrusion, role conflict or role spill-over. We need to understand how the demands of one role intrude upon the other and along
what dimensions these intrusions tend to occur -- e.g., time,
emotion, attention, physical energy.

Pleck (1977) presents some insights regarding the interface of
the two roles. He suggests the presence of asymmetrically permeable
boundaries between work and family for the two sexes. For women,
the family role is allowed to intrude upon work. In general, women
have to leave work to take care of sick children or attend school
functions. On the other hand, dinner may be delayed or weekend
activities cancelled because men are detained by work activities.
The implications of Pleck's hypothesis deserve research attention.
Hall (1972) presents another researchable hypothesis. He suggests
that men who work and have a family have two sequential roles,
whereas women who work and have a family have two simultaneous
roles. In contrast to men's family responsibilities which can be
handled during the evening, women's family responsibilities continue
throughout the day. Women, therefore, should experience more role

overload (too many role demands at the same time) and role conflict
(different or opposing demands from different roles) than men do.

Research should also look into the job-related and family-rela-
ted correlates of role intrusions or conflicts, and how these affect
individual, family and job outcomes. There has been extensive, but
dated, psychological research on the effects of work on family.
These studies have tended to focus on the mere fact of women's employment on their families, with no concern for the conditions of
employment. Little or no research on this issue has focused on men,
since much of the research had an implicit assumption that employment of women was an anomaly that interfered with the performance of
their proper functions in the home. For both women and men, it is
important to investigate the specific characteristics of the work
situation -- e.g., work schedules, and number of working hours, job
pressures, job opportunities, supervisory relationships -- on the
extent of work-family conflicts and on behavior and affect in the
family setting.

The effects of family demands and characteristics on work-family
conflicts and on work behaviors should also be of interest to researchers and managers. How do family demands affect job-related
outcomes such as job satisfaction, motivation and turnover? Very
little empirical data exists in this area. A preliminary analysis
of a Navy data set (Nieva, 1979) showed that, indeed, family demands
affected job outcomes, and they do so differentially -- they
affected satisfaction and intention to stay in the organization but
did not affect effort exerted on the job. The pattern of results is
in line with other I/O findings that, contrary to expectations, the
factors affecting retention and satisfaction differ from those
affecting motivation.

These questions can be given a slightly different twist if questions are phrased in terms of role reinforcements. For example, one
might ask, how do families support an employee's job related activities? The traditional example of the corporate wife comes to mind
here, but new models of support might be identified given changing
family forms and functions. Other related questions might also be
asked -- how important are various types of family support, e.g.,
instrumental versus emotional support, to an individual's
performance on the job?

Kanter (1977) suggests that people tend to downplay the connections between work and family. Furthermore, current organizational
philosophies tend to operate under the assumption of separate
worlds, disclaiming responsibility for the family lives of their
members, while implicitly making demands that affect the lives of
the families of their employees. Research should address the rights
of organizations to make such demands of employees and their families and what the benefits and costs are to families in such

positions. It should look into the work characteristics -- both job and organizational structures -- that "consume" workers, leaving them "burnt out" for their personal lives. Conversely, what do organizations owe the families of their workers on whom they place such high demands? It would be interesting for research to look into management beliefs on what the relationships between work organizations and employee families should be, and on corporate responsibilities for employee families; contrasting these with employee perceptions of actual and desired corporate role in their private lives. Other questions may be of interest to both management and employees. What payoffs do organizations see in helping their employees cope with work-family issues? How can work systems be designed so as to allow effective participation in both worlds?

At the present time, most employers do not consider the welfare of their employees as family members to be an organizational concern. Company policies and practices, therefore, are often designed and enforced as though the employees either had no competing concerns or that responsibilities outside their jobs are naturally subordinate to their work demand. Interesting outcomes might occur if companies were to consider their employees as members of families and to take that seriously into their policy-making. Special provisions may emerge, such as are represented in the accounts of some small companies that, in effect, have decided that the best thing that could happen to the company would be for the families of its employees to see it as a direct source of the family's well being. Many jobs can be done in the home. These jobs range from stuffing envelopes, to operating computer terminals for tasks such as word processing, data analysis, or confirming airplane reservations. On the other hand, the workplace could take on a homey atmosphere. One unusual account, for example, describes a workplace that contains a quasi-country club with swimming pool and courts for spouses and children to play, and where the employees could more easily join their families in the middle of the work day. This minimizes the segmentation that most workers experience between their work and home lives.

Less dramatic than such developments, and perhaps more generally achievable are changes within the work-benefit structures that already exist. The form of benefits that most companies regularly give their employees is an obvious place to start. Already companies have assumed responsibilities for health care. Could companies conceive it consistent with their long range interest to go beyond this to institute such benefits as child day care? This innovation has already been adapted by a number of organizations, and it would be of interest to look into the costs and benefits of building in daycare services for employees. Child care is a family demand that most regularly poses conflict between work and family interests. This is particularly true in the single-parent headed family when there is no other person available to assume or share responsibility for child care. Other benefits related to family duties could be designed for male employees that would have indirect benefits to their spouses. One such benefit would be the allocation of paternity leave, which has a precedent in Scandinavian countries. This would recognize the joint parental responsibility, particularly immediately after birth of the child.

There are some indications of exploration among employers that could be particularly beneficial for the worker who also has family responsibilities (cf. Davis and Taylor, 1979). One development is flexible working hours. Flexitime, in many variations, has been adopted in a large number of bureaucracies and factories, with generally favorable reactions by both management and the ordinary employee. Another innovation finding some acceptance, that merits investigation, is the concept of shared jobs. It is conventional wisdom that many jobs cannot be split and that adequate work accountability is possible if only one person is responsible. This tradition is, however, coming under increasing review from many in the work-redesign area. Another variation, actually an old idea, is the part-time job. Given the way family and society are structured today, many women have to limit themselves to part-time jobs in order to fulfill their marital and parental responsibilities. This also limits the jobs they can obtain largely to low skill, low responsibility, low income types, with little potential for upward mobility. These jobs are also frequently limited in the accrual of benefits (such as vacation, tenure, retirement) that are typically assumed as rights by the full-time employee. Greater legitimacy for part-time jobs would enable more women to simultaneously manage family and work requirements. The presence of full-time and part-time jobs, however, makes it difficult to eliminate status differences -- full-time jobs for males may always be the "better" jobs than part-time jobs for females. An ongoing discussion on work policies in Sweden expands the notion of altering all work schedules from eight to six hour jobs. Such an arrangement would allow more time for all employees to fulfill both work and family obligations, and would eliminate any possible stigma accompanying less than full time work. Any of these variations in work arrangements are replete with difficulties and complexities and clearly suggest the necessity of careful research.

Other general and perhaps more basic inquiries are stimulated by the need to understand better the relationships between family and work. We need to pay more serious attention to the old concept of "partial inclusion" (Allport, 1933) -- the segmental involvement of people in social groupings including work organizations. A related concept, though with a somewhat different emphasis, is "occupational absorptiveness" -- i.e., the extent to which one's work draws in and makes demands upon other family members (Parker, 1967). We need to understand what characteristics of the job, occupation and work organization make work conditions more or less absorptive and what work absorptiveness means for employees and their families.

One can expand the question of work absorptiveness to a more general inquiry as to the distance or separateness of the work and family spheres. In what kinds of jobs or occupations are they most closely tied together -- therefore making it more important to consider the ways that each sphere affects the other -- and where are they most separate? What are the implications of varying degrees of separation on work and family? It would be useful to consider the work-family issues just discussed within a two by two matrix, defined by separateness between work and family and dominance of one sphere over the other.

While we are interested in general statements about the interface of work and family, in-depth understanding will come only by dealing with specific work situations (e.g., professional and blue collar workers) and specific family situations (e.g., single parent, couples, dual-career couples and childless couples). Studying unique family-work combinations will enable us to understand nuances of the work-family relationship. As examples, I will focus on two types of situations -- the dual career couple and the single parent.

Family-work issues have received some attention in recent research on dual-career couples. For example, Epstein (1971) looked at the division of labor at work and at home among lawyer couples; Poloma (1977) and Garland (1972) examined role conflicts and resolutions for both husbands and wives in dual-career couples; and Bryson et. al (1976) have examined the professional productivity of dual career couples.

However, many issues remain untouched. For example, how do dual career couples handle simultaneous job pressures or demands? How does one define the "best solution" in situations of conflict -- in terms of an "average good," "least harm" or some other definition? What support mechanisms can they develop to substitute for the lack of a full-time nurturer and child caretaker? How do job demands of one affect the job performance of the other partner? Are there differences in work or family processes depending on the couple's stage in the family life cycle and in the career stage of each person?

From an institutional point of view, it also becomes increasingly important to consider the needs of dual-career couples and to consider optimal institutional responses to their needs. Work organizations need basic information to guide their actions. How do dual-career couples differ from others in their responses to institutional demands, particularly demands for mobility and travel? What kinds of benefits would be appropriate to these couples? As the dual-career pattern becomes more prevalent, particularly in certain professions, work institutions may be faced with new concerns. Is it a good strategy to employ both partners, or under what conditions would such an arrangement be advantageous? Do innovations such as "shared jobs" for couples benefit company interests?

Companies may also be faced with new dilemmas. How does one reconcile, for example, the need to be responsive to dual-career "pack-
ages" where employment for both husband and wife is desired, with
requirements for open job advertising and selection purely on quali-
fications?

A second group of interest is single parents, most of whom are
women. Some research is starting to accumulate on this ever increasing segment of the population (e.g., Ross and Sawhill, 1975;
Brandwein, Brown and Fox, 1974; Campbell, Converse and Rodgers,
1976, pp. 419-421). These women are underprivileged in every sense
of the word; they are overburdened with repsonsibilities, have
little security and scarce resources; only one-third feel confident
that they can meet their expenses (Campbell, et al., 1976). At
least half of women heads of families had median incomes below the
poverty level.

It is obvious that the family-work problems that single parents
face are very different from those confronted by dual-career
couples. Problems of single parents are often economic (e.g., inadequate incomes to provide for the family)(Corcoran and Duncan,
1979) and psychological (e.g., inadequate social support to handle
all the problems of work and parent roles)(Giele, 1978). What support systems are available to them and what coping mechanisms can
they develop? Single parents do not prepare for their roles in the
way dual-career couples do because most people do not aspire to become single parents. Often acquiring the status by unforeseen circumstances, single parents, are often ill-prepared to assume the
roles of solo parent and solo worker. Does their lack of prepared-
ness and economic insecurity make them more vulnerable to exploitation or harassment at work?

Alternative work and career patterns Most adult women with
families will be in the labor force for significant periods of time.
In fact, the time is approaching (or may have already come) when the
woman who is not employed outside the home becomes both statistically and normatively deviant. However, unless or until family
responsibilities are no longer primarily/automatically assigned to
women, women's behavioral attachment to the labor force will differ
somewhat from men's. We lack vital information on how women move
through the labor force over the life cycle. What are the important
transition points in the relationships between work/career, marriage
and childbearing, and what are the choices perceived at various
transition points? The literature identifies several general descriptions of career patterns that provide useful starting points.
For example, Super (1957) and Cooper (1963) identified three types
of career patterns: 1) the one role pattern, in which the work and
domestic roles are sequential, the young woman working in a stop-gap
job until she marries and leaves the labor force; 2) the interrupted
pattern in which a one role and a two role pattern may involve

taking time off to rear children and then return to uninterrupted
employment; 3) an unstable in-and-out of the labor force pattern
that fits her short term needs or personal whims. Bernard (1971)
discussed career patterns of professional women, involving various
combinations of marriage, childbearing, career preparation, and
career work, e.g., an early interrupted, late interrupted or uninterrupted patterns. We know very little, however, about the processes behind and the consequences of such different patterns on
achievement at work, and on the individual's personal well-being.

The study of work histories over time can address a number of
basic questions: How important is a continuous attachment to the
labor force in terms of later achievements and status? At what
points are interruptions most detrimental, and for what kinds of
jobs/occupations? What kinds of activities during periods of interruptions can be designed to be beneficial to later work status
(an obvious one here is a return to school, but there must be
others)? How does timing and length of interruption affect
re-entry?

The study of women's work histories must go beyond the more
limited questions of why women decide to enter and leave the labor
force -- a focus on employment decisions -- to a concern with how
they build or develop careers; realizing that, for many, there may
be interruptions along the way. The notion of a future orientation,
a continued interest in work and career progression has been almost
completely absent in the examination of women's work histories. On
the other hand, the study of careers, which has been typically taken
to be a male concern (Schein, 1978), has usually assumed a continuous pattern, with no major detours.

Developing definitions of careers different from the traditional
continuous model will be important to understanding many women's,
and increasingly many men's, work behavior. Here it is essential to
consider the intersections of the work/career cycle and the family
cycle, and to examine the allocation of time and energy along longitudinal lines. Research in life cycles has begun to uncover important patterns for men (e.g., Levinson, 1978), and this kind of inquiry should be expanded to women as well.

Schein (1978) presents a perspective that provides a useful
starting point for gathering data on parallel life cycles, including
work. He visualizes the situation as in Figure 1, which shows a
biosocial life cycle, a work/career cycle and a family procreation
cycle. Each has its own tasks and choices, and the simultaneous
occurrence of difficult tasks in more than one cycle presents the
greatest difficulty as well as the greatest opportunity for radical
growth. The life cycle perspective emphasizes questions of timing
and the number and difficulty of tasks at particular points in time.

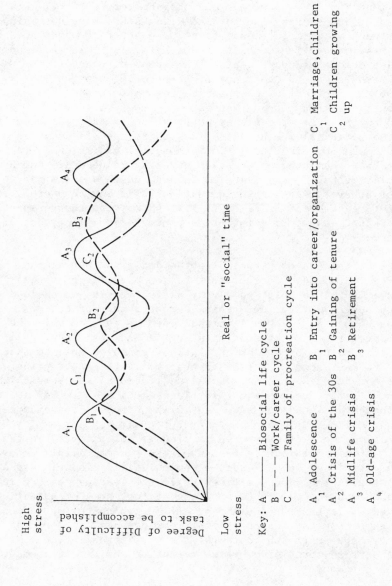

Figure 1. A model of life/career/family interaction (taken from Schein, 1978)

It would be instructive to examine in closer detail specific junctures and time periods along the career/life cycle. One such transition point is the decision to re-enter the labor force after a period of interruption. How does one prepare for re-entry? What is the process of job search like for individuals who have not maintained active ties with the labor force? Re-entering women need information, assistance in assessing themselves vis-a-vis the labor market and emotional support during the period of transition. Many questions revolve around the needs of re-entering women. What kinds of alternative institutions can provide for these needs? To what extent should these supporting mechanisms come from formal institutions, and to what extent can they be provided by informal networks available to potential re-entrants? Are there specific populations of women who are most isolated from both formal and informal resources and for whom special outreach efforts are needed? Which problems of re-entering women are unique and which are similar to problems of other populations or situations. It may be useful, for example, for researchers of re-entry issues to adapt the perspective of career change, e.g., from full-time homemaker to employment or from volunteer to paid work.

Another transition point would be the decision to leave an existing work situation, whether this be for a temporary recess from formal employment or a shift to a very different kind of employment. Information on the motivations behind career interruptions or changes may be useful to organizational efforts to keep valued employees. Given the high cost of breaking in and training new employees, it is to the organization's advantage to be able to design mechanisms to meet some of the needs that motivate interrupting attachment to the organization. Some institutional mechanisms like this already exist, such as maternity leave policies. Other mechanisms, although designed for other specific purposes, are examples of devices to allow employees to interrupt their regular employment without leaving their primary organizations. For example, in the government sector, interagency personnel assignments allow employees to acquire experience in different agencies, giving individuals a chance to broaden their perspectives while not leaving their home institution permanently. In the private sector, some organizations have allowed employees to take a year off for volunteer or community service work without an interruption in employment. Although such measures may have short-run costs for the work organization, there may be pay-offs in terms of employee retention, skill enhancement, and reduced burn-out.

Research should also look into the feasibility of alternative policies around planned interruptions. For example, can seniority policies be designed so that employees can pick up where they left off, if the interruption does not exceed a certain length of time? Can organizational policies be designed to enable the individual and the organization to maintain contact, if desired by either party, so

that skills are maintained and re-entry difficulties are minimized?
This is presently done informally, but institutionalized procedures
may help maintain women in the work force who would otherwise drop
out involuntarily.

In general one might expect the pattern of interrupted work patterns to rise with the increase of dual-worker and dual-career
couples. With the burden of producing income taken on by both husband and wife, there is increased freedom for men to develop alternate uses of time, to take a break from formal employment or to take
time to change to a more attractive field of endeavor. Breaks in
labor force attachment (without a necessary break in career attachment) may be necessary at certain points in time if desirable opportunities are not available simultaneously for both partners. Thus
far most of the interruptions and accommodations have affected wives
rather than husbands in dual-career couples, but this too may change
with increases in egalitarian values for couples. Research should
look into the changing patterns of career strategies of dual-career
couples.

The possibility of interruptions in one's formal connections to
the labor force brings into question new definitions of career commitment and labor force attachment. Traditional measures of work
commitment should incorporate the notion of voluntary interruptions
of formal employment without a necessary interruption of career commitment. The assumption of a continuous involvement in a line of
work for which one received formal training early on is already outdated, given the realities of fast changing technology. It becomes
even more outdated when one considers seriously the changes implied
by having two income producers in the family, particularly if the
income gap between the partners becomes narrower with more equity in
the workplace.

Increasing Parity Between Men and Women in the Labor Force

Towards Desegregating Occupations. Perhaps the biggest barrier
to parity between men and women in the labor force is occupational
sex-segregation. Most women are still found in a small number of
over-crowded lower paying occupations (Oppenheimer, 1968; Shrank &
Riley 1975). And even within occupational groupings, segregation
remains substantial. For example, among sales workers, men were
likely to be in high paying, commissioned, non-retail jobs, while
women were in the lower paying retail trade (U.S. Department of
Labor, 1976).

A basic problem, therefore, is breaking down occupational barriers between the sexes. Although legislation has removed legal ob-
stacles to the sex integration of jobs, more information is needed
to facilitate the movement of women into higher paying male jobs and
to make their acceptance in the work place an attainable objective.

One can mold a number of perspectives in this effort. A psychological bias would be to formulate the problem in terms of individuals
-- i.e., the woman "pioneer", her co-workers, or her supervisor.
From this viewpoint, it is important to investigate the attitudinal,
perceptual, ability and personality factors that affect the choice
of occupation and the effective functioning of females in traditionally male occupations (or vice versa). Research on women from
this perspective has been ample and wide ranging, including attention to a variety of issues, e.g., fear of success, masculinity-
femininity, self-esteem, and family (vs. career) orientation. There
has been some, though much less, attention to the influence of co-
workers and supervisors on the integration of women at work. Thus
far relevant studies of co-workers and supervisors have focused
largely on sexrole attitudes and attitudes toward women workers or
managers. Research should go beyond these topics. Some useful
avenues might be investigations into consequences anticipated from
the sex-integration process, including loss of prestige, or
slackening of standards. Further, research along these lines should
overcome some of its bias towards the study of professionals and
college students. We know very little about women's entry into
male-dominated non-professional jobs such as carpentry or construction. This kind of research is only beginning and represents a
critical area of development.

An area where useful contributions have already been made by I/O
psychologists is in the detection of bias or non-job relatedness in
testing devices. Work on validating existing tests in terms of
their ability to predict job performance has already proven useful
in breaking down occupational sex barriers to some extent. There is
much room and need for the development of new devices that are valid
(i.e., predictive of actual job performance), unbiased, and logis-
tically feasible. A related avenue, also well travelled by I/O
practitioners and researchers, is the assessment of "true" job requirements. Numerous job evaluation systems exist, focusing on different aspects of job requirements, e.g., physical strength, skill
requirements, and mental processing. Knowing the technology exists,
it would be interesting to find out how many and which organizations
and occupations employ these systems, and to what extent instituting
such systems (where they have not been traditionally used) actually
increases the number of women in male-dominated work.

A general issue that has been inadequately explored by I/O
psychologists is the effects that various structural characteristics
of organizations or occupations have on the ease or difficulty of
breaking down sex-segregation at work. Kanter (1977) and other researchers (e.g., Taylor, et al., 1978) emphasize the importance of
relative numbers or sex ratios in breaking occupational barriers
between the sexes. Research has shown that "solos" or "tokens" have
problems that are directly attributable to their rarity. The issue
of numbers needs more exploration. If women are scattered through-

out the traditionally male organization or occupation, they suffer
pressure from excessive visibility and isolation. Yet, it is also
important that women do not form other "pink ghettos" that isolate
them as a group from the mainstream. The strategy for increasing
the number of women in traditionally male occupations must be worked
out carefully. In particular, research can be helpful in understanding the conditions under which backlash can occur and, conversely, the conditions which would facilitate the acceptance of
non-traditional employees.

The issue of relative numbers may also have implications for the
occupation or work organization which is newly opened to women.
Experimental evidence (Touhey, 1974) suggests that increasing the
number of women in a high-status male occupation has the effect of
lowering its perceived prestige. Would this be borne out in the
real world? Under what conditions does lowered prestige imply
lowered wages as well? The classic historical example is the prestige loss suffered by the bank teller job when it shifted from being
a male to a female job.

Research would also be helpful in identifying other characteristics of occupations or organizations that facilitate or impede
sexual integration. One such element might be the degree of interdependence in the work situation, which determines the extent to
which interaction is important at work. It seems plausible to suggest that when interdependence requirements are low, employees can
function relatively autonomously, whereas when they are high, positive relationships among co-workers become essential.

One might also look into the effects of "stage in the sex-integration process" on the extent or difficulty of sex-integration.
Sex-integration is basically a process of innovation and change, and
variables that are important for sex-integration may differ at various stages of the process. For example, femininity may be important for initial acceptance but may be inconsequential at later
stages.

Another such element is the role of sexuality in the workplace.
This issue has at least two major components worth research attention. One is the fear of sexuality at work as a barrier to integrating male-dominated occupations, such as the military, police
work and trucking; a phenomenon that has been widely documented in
anecdotal journalistic writing but has received hardly any empirical
attention. One unique study (Quinn, 1978) found that, indeed, many
fears existed around the issue of workplace sexuality and that there
was some foundation for such fears in that negative consequences for
both men and women were seen as the result of sexual liaisons at work.

Another component of sexuality at work has received much recent
attention -- the exploitation of women's sexuality or sexual harass-

ment (Farley, 1978; Mackinnon, 1979). How much is sexual harassment used as a way to keep women out or to make them so uncomfortable that they leave? Although declared illegal by recent regulations of the EEOC, there is no consensus, as yet, on the definition of sexual harassment. Definitional efforts as well as research into the work-related consequences of sexual harassment at the workplace should receive increasing attention as more women enter the work force. Some consequences are clear, such as making sexual compliance an explicit condition of employment or promotion; others are less so. Recent EEOC guidelines say that "when verbal or physical conduct has the effect -- intentionally or unintentionally -- of creating an intimidating, offensive or hostile work environment which could ultimately affect a person's work performance" (Sec. 1604.11) this could constitute harassment. The legal and research establishments should work together to clarify this statement. Further, more thought will be given to institutional vs individual responsibilities for reducing sexual harassment at work. The EEOC guidelines state that the employer is held responsible if a supervisor or even a co-worker engages in sexual harassment. Therefore, it would be in the organization's interests to understand better what conditions create an atmosphere that encourages or discourages sexual harassment, and what kind of work structures and procedures can be developed to minimize such incidents.

Upgrading women's jobs Even with increased impetus towards female employment in traditionally male jobs, it is likely that the majority of women will be working in "female" occupations. Thus, it is critical to search for ways to upgrade female-dominated jobs. In fact, this issue may be more important than opening access to traditionally male jobs in terms of the number of women who will be affected.

One type of change that would improve parity in the rewards received by working men and women without altering the segregated occupational structures is the push for equal pay for work of equal value. The limitations of the axiom "equal pay for equal work" are evident when one sees the lower wages given to the traditionally female nursing job, for example, in comparison to the traditionally male assembly worker job. Arguments that the market should be left alone to determine wages for different occupations fall apart in the face of manipulations of free market forces by unions and other mechanisms. Clearly the assessment of what constitutes work of equal value is a complicated problem, and in the end there has to be agreement on the subjective core of the matter: what constitutes "value" or "worth". Analyses of "work of equal value" inevitably requires a value judgment on the relative worth of such diverse job requirements as strength vs. training or skill vs. accountability. Job evaluation systems often emphasize functions that favor male oriented jobs. The National Academy of Science, commissioned by the

EEOC to study the issue of comparable worth (NAS, 1979) gave an example:

> ...manual skill factors stress ability to handle
> tools rather than dexterity, which has the effect
> of downgrading fine assembly work, done largely
> by women.

Thus there is a need to examine the subtle emphasis given various factors in job evaluation systems for potential bias and also to consider how various abstract factors are operationalized in the assessment devices.

In addition to wages, changes in other aspects of women's jobs may serve as means of upgrading. Research might try to identify where these levers are. One such change could be to define women's jobs in such a way as to allow direct rather than vicarious achievements, evaluations and rewards (cf. Barrett, 1979). The secretarial job is the classic case in point, where frequently salary levels are set by the level of the secretary's boss rather than by the difficulty of the secretary's job. Another change, also well-illustrated by the case of the secretary, is the delineation of specific job duties which moves the job away from one of generalized service to a more professional definition.

A critical feature of present women's jobs is limited upward mobility -- women's jobs are often dead-end jobs. In many cases these jobs provide much important experience that goes unrecognized -- how many times have we jokingly said that secretaries actually run their offices? Job analyses should be conducted on the secretarial and other typically women's jobs to establish linkages with other job categories for which the skills developed are required changes in opportunity structures in work organizations are necessary to get women out of their dead-end situations. Such changes will depend heavily once again on thorough reassessment of the true requirements of jobs in order to reduce the artificial truncation that presently characterize many female job ladders.

Obtaining power and authority. Although the number of women in the workforce has been increasing steadily in the recent past, very few occupy positions of power or leadership in the workplace. National statistics show that women tend to be concentrated at the bottom of most organizations (U.S. Department of Labor, 1976) and studies (e.g., Miner, 1974, Roussell, 1974) show consistently that women lag behind men in terms of upward mobility, and that the lag cannot be accounted for by rational factors such as education and experience (e.g., Malkiel & Malkiel, 1973; Astin & Bayer, 1972). Even when women have the same formal titles, they have been found to have less autonomy and influence (Hansen, 1974; Goetz & Herman, 1976) than their male colleagues.

In an earlier paper (Nieva, 1978) I suggested that the many studies of women and leadership, in following traditional leadership research paradigms, have missed the critical differentiator between the sexes -- power. Studies have shown no consistent sex differences in leadership traits or styles, but it appears, from limited data, that power makes the difference.

The concept of power is a familiar one in the world of work and organizations, yet issues such as how it is manifested and how it is acquired are insufficiently understood. Kanter (1977) provides a useful and organizationally relevant definition -- it is "the ability to get things done, to mobilize resources, to get and to use whatever it is that a person needs for the goals he or she is attempting to meet" (p. 166). This definition emphasizes mastery, the power to do. Related to this is the power to make others do, particularly if these "others" are the resources that have to be utilized. Better understanding of the concept of organizational power will provide insight into the subtle differences between the positions of men and women in work organizations, and should provide another way of defining parity at work.

An important organizational characteristic to study in relation to power at work is the operation and location of informal "ceilings" in the organization. As access becomes more equitable at entry levels, research attention should shift increasingly to mobility blockages. Will women who have been allowed in, "top out"? One avenue by which this phenomenon can be explored is through the identification and description of job ladders in the workplace. For some jobs, such as the secretarial positions discussed, it is clear that ladders are virtually non-existent. However, for many jobs mobility ladders are less obvious and there may be different ones for men and women. Research on person perception and evaluation provides other leads for understanding the subtle operation of "ceilings" for women. Although ample evidence of sex-related bias across many situations has been accummulated, the situation appears to be aggravated by the level of the position or the excellence of performance being evaluated (Nieva & Gutek, 1980). There are strong tendencies to dole out extra penalties to more competent women than to incompetent or mediocre women and the pro-male bias seems greater in demanding than in routine jobs. the effect of level is exacerbated by the inherent ambiguity and lack of clear standards characterizing many higher level positions.

The costs that accompany women in higher level positions is an important issue to explore. Do these costs differ depending on the type of occupation? Are they different for women moving up from within and for women coming in from outside? How do "fast-track" women relate to slower moving male and female colleagues? Can organizations build in supports so that individual and organizational costs are minimized? We would hope that the Mary Cunningham

syndrome does not repeat itself too often as women begin to have
opportunities to rise.

Further research on the role of the token is another avenue to
understanding the opportunities for mobility and power. The token
is an individual who is provided rewards and credentials not allowed
others with similar statuses. The extent to which real opportunities are becoming available to women must be assessed against the
alternative possible situation of tokenism. Research efforts to
define the dimensions of tokenism in operational and measurable
terms can provide indices for assessing organizational opportunities
for women. Effort should also be made to try to identify the
effects of tokenism on individual behaviors. To what extent does
having a token provide a motivating role model for others in the
organization? To what extent does it raise false hopes that, when
disillusioned, depress the aspirations of women even further? Can a
token position be identified before one is in it, and how can it be
turned into a positive force for others in the organization? Research must identify both individual and organizational aspects of
tokenism.

Effects of a declining economy. Economic studies show that
women workers have suffered more than men in past economic downturns
(cf. Smith 1979). A general decline in economic growth in the near
future could be more detrimental to women with increasing numbers of
women coming into the labor force. Researchers should be ready to
address the problems accompanying a shrinking pie for which there
are growing numbers of claimants.

One task is largely descriptive. How are allocation decisions
made when times are tight? Researchers could shed light on the influence of surplus and scarcity on people's value hierarchies. How
strongly, for example, would people and institutions hold on to
equal opportunity values, when other values seem threatened? Is
equal opportunity a concept born out of affluence? How much do
women and men, managers and others differ on this issue? Another
kind of inquiry could focus on specific kinds of allocation decisions to assess how they are affected by surplus and scarcity conditions. It may be possible to determine whether changing conditions
have greater effects on decisions regarding access, promotions/mob-
ility opportunities, or termination. Still another kind of inquiry
could look into differential effects among various populations defined by demographics, occupations, level in the hierarchy, size of
organization, etc. It will be important to identify the "most
affected" groups in order to identify remedies that could be targeted to them.

An important general concern especially in the face of a general
decline is ensuring that equalization of opportunity between men and
women not be seen as lessening the opportunities of men. Already we

have seen battles over issues of reverse discrimination and affirmative action quotas. It may be that such resistance is more likely
as long as remedies are presented in ways that focus on men and
women as identified groups. Emphasis on differentiation can be expected to heighten intergroup consciousness, and may serve to over-
accentuate possible adversarial interests of the two groups.

I/O researchers should search for innovative ways of dealing
with a fixed or shrinking pie. With a fixed need for a certain number of hours to be worked, for example, is it feasible to allocate
them in ways other than the traditional week? As mentioned earlier,
Sweden is debating the shorter workday for both sexes to allow better performance of both work and family roles. The same solution
may apply to the fixed pie problem. What conditions would pave the
way to the acceptance of such an innovation? Research might provide
some answers. I would suggest that (in chicken and egg fashion) the
more women work and the more progress they have made towards occupational equity, the more likely it would be that shortened workdays
would be welcomed by both sexes.

It may well be again the case here that it is not sufficient to
be bounded by the work world in looking for solutions to the effects
of decline. If a shrinking occupational pie is a given, at least
for some periods of time, and women continue to push for equal
treatment in the workplace, some degree of displacement of traditional workers may be inevitable. Who would these traditional workers be? If there is truth to the ideal of meritocracy, it is likely
that these would include less-able men who would be negatively
affected by the removal of barriers for women that served to protect
the men in the past. We may have "displaced workers," mostly male,
as the counterpart to the "displaced homemakers" who are female.
For displaced male workers, there would be benefits derived from
social changes that move away from defining the work world (with
attendant rights and responsibilities) as male and the world of the
family as female. It may become more and more important for increasing numbers of men to be able to develop sources of identify,
security and fulfillment outside of the world of work.

Concluding Remarks

If researchers pay serious attention to the increasing feminini-
zation of the labor force, many issues present themselves for examination. I have focused on a few major ones, suggested by the persisting inequities between the conditions faced by men and women who
work. In addressing any of these issues, there are a number of research tasks for the I/O psychologist. Descriptive studies of
changing conditions must be conducted to keep our pictures of reality accurate, and to inform our prescriptions for change.
Descriptive studies also do much to redefine our concepts of what to
consider problemmatic, and the extent to which certain types of
occurrences merit further attention.

In addition to descriptive studies, we need to conduct research on the antecedents and consequences of behaviors of concern, and to be able to use these explanations to design alternatives for creating change. In general, there have been four types of explanatory variables used in most of the relevant literature thus far -- individual level variables (research assumes that individual characteristics underlie behaviors, e.g., achievement and leadership); structural-institutional variables (research focuses on the impact that work organizations have on the people in them, and looks at how people reflect their situations in their behavior); sex-role variables (research focuses on behaviors defined as appropriate or inappropriate for each sex) and power variables (research focuses on the power differential between men and women in various situations). Each kind of explanation uncovers part of the picture, and each suggests a different lever for effecting change. In designing research or change efforts one has to be aware of the choices that one is making among these variables. One also has to be aware of the relationships among these classes of variables, and in particular, that changes in one set requires and implies changes in the others. The increasing participation of women in the labor force is clearly one of the most important social changes in modern times. It has important implications not only for the behaviors of individual men and women as they function in various life spheres but also for the institutional structures that they inhabit.

References

Allport, F. H., Institutional behavior. Chapel Hill, N.C., University of North Carolina Press, 1933.

Astin H., & Bayer, A. Sex discrimination in academe. Educational Record, 1972, 54, 101-118.

Bailyn L., & Schein, E. H. Life/career conditions as indicators of quality of employment. In A. D. Biderman and T. F. Drury (Eds.), Measuring work quality for social reporting. Beverly Hills, CA: Sage 1976.

Barrett, N. S. Women in the job market: Occupations, earnings and career opportunities. In R. Smith (Ed.)., The subtle revolution, Washington, D.C.: The Urban Institute, 1979.

Brandwein, R. A., Brown, C. A., & Fox, E. M. Women and children last: The social situation of divorced mothers and their families. Journal of Marriage and the Family, 1974, 36, 498-515.

Bryson, R. B., Bryson, J. B., Licht, M. H., & Licht, B. G. The professional pair: Husband and wife psychologists. American Psychologist, 1976, 31, 10-16.

Campbell, A., Converse, P., & Rodgers, W. The quality of american life, New York: Russell Sage, 1976.

Cooper, S. Career patterns of women. Vocational Rehabilitation and Education Quarterly, 1963, 13-14, 21-28.

Corcoran, M., & Duncan, G. Work history, labor force attachment and earnings differences between the races and sexes. The Journal of Human Resources, 1979, 14, 3-20.

Davis, L. E., & Taylor, J. C. Design of jobs. Santa Monica: Good-
    year Publishing Co., 1979.

Epstein, C. F. Law partners and marital partners: Strains and
    solutions in the dual career family enterprise. Human
    Relations, 1971, 24, 549-564.

Farley, L. Sexual shakedown. New York: McGraw-Hill, 1978.

Flaim, P. O., & Fullerton, H. N., Labor force projections to 1990:
    Three possible paths. Montly Labor Review, 1978, 25-35.

Garland, N. T. The better half? The male in the dual professional
    family in C. Safilivos-Rothchild's (Ed.), Toward a sociology of
    women. Lexington, Mass.: Xerox, 1972.

Gartner, A., & Reissman, F. Is there a new work ethic? American
    Journal of Orthopsychiatry, 1974, 44, 563-619.

Giele, J. Women and the future. New York: Free Press, 1978.

Goetz, T. E., & Herman, J. B. Effects of supervisors' and subordi-
    nates' sex on productivity and morale. Paper presented at the
    American Psychological Association 84th annual convention,
    Washington, D.C. September 1976.

Gordon, F., & Strober, M. (Eds.). Bringing women into management.
    New York: McGraw-Hill, 1975.

Grossman, A. S. Special labor-force reports summaries: Divorces
    and separated women in the labor force -- an update. Monthly
    Labor Review, 1978, 101(10), 43-45.

Gutek, B. A., Nakamura, C., & Nieva, V. F. Work and family inter-
    dependencies. Journal of Occupational Behavior, 1981, 2, 1-16.

Hall, D. T. A model of coping with role conflict: the role
    behavior of college educated women. Administrative Science
    Quarterly, 1972, 17, 471-486.

Hansen, D. Sex differences and supervision. Paper presented at the
    American Psychological Association, New Orleans 1974.

Hennig, M., & Jardim, A. The managerial women. New York:
    Doubleday, 1977.

Kanter, R. M. Work and family in the United States: A critical
    review and agenda for research. New York: Russell Sage, 1977.

MacKinnon, C. A. Sexual harassment of working women. New Haven:
    Yale University Press, 1979.

Malkiel, B. G., & Malkiel, J. A. Male-female pay differentials in
    professional employment. American Economic Review, 1973, 63,
    693-704.

Mason, K. O., Czaka, J. L., & Arber, S. Change in U.S. women's sex
    role attitudes. American Sociological Review, 1976, 4, 574-596.

Miner, J. B. Motivation to manage among women: Studies of business
    managers and educational administrators. Journal of Vocational
    Behavior, 1974, 5, 197-208.

Nieva, V. F. The family's impact on job-related attitudes of women
    and men: report of work in progress. Paper presented at the
    annual convention of the American Psychological Association, New
    York, 1979.

Nieva, V. F. Women and leadership: Research to date. Annual Conference of the Association of Women in Psychology, Pittsburgh, 1978; and American Psychological Association, Toronto, 1978.

Nieva, V. F., & Gutek, B. A. Sex effects in evaluation. The Academy of Management Review, 1980, 5, 267-276.

Oppenheimer, V. The sex labelling of jobs. Industrial Relations, 1968, 7, 219-234.

Parker, S. R. Industry and the family. In Sociology of industry, New York: Praeger, 1967.

Pleck, J. H. The work-family role system. Social Problems, 1977, 24, 417-427.

Poloma, M. M. Role conflict and the married professional woman. In C. Safilios-Rothschild (ed.). Toward a sociology of women, Lexington, Mass: Xerox 1972.

Quinn, R. Coping with cupid: The formation, impact and management of romantic relationships in organizations, Administrative Science Quarterly, 1977, 22, 30-45.

Ross, H. L., & Sawhill, I. Time of transition. Washington, D.C.: The Urban Institute, 1975.

Roussell, C. Relationship of sex of department head to department climate. Administrative Science Quarterly, 1974, 19, 211-220.

Schein, E. H. Career dynamics: Matching individual and organizational needs, Reading, Mass: Addison-Wesley, 1978.

Schrank, T. H., & Riley, J. W. Women on work organizations. In J. M. Kreps (ed.), Women and the American economy. Englewood Cliffs: Prentice Hall, 1975.

Smith, R. E. Women in the labor force in 1990. An Urban Institute working paper UI-1156-1, Washington, D.C.: The Urban Institute, 1979.

Stewart, J. Review essay, Administrative Science Quarterly, 1978, 23, 336-350.

Super, D. The psychology of careers. New York: Harper and Row, 1957.

Taylor, S. E., Fiske, S. T., Etcoff, N. L., & Ruderman, A. J. Categorical and contextual basis of person memory and stereotyping. Journal of Personality and Social Psychology, 1978, 36, 778-793.

Touhey, J. C. Effects of additional women professionals on ratings of occupational prestige and desirability. Journal of Personality and Social Psychology, 1974, 29, 86-89.

U.S. Department of Labor, Employment and Training Administration, Employment and training report of the President, 1978, 205-219.

U.S. Department of Labor, 1975 handbook on women workers, Washington, D.C., 1976.

COMMENTARY ON STUDIES OF GENDER-MIX

IN LABOR MARKET RESEARCH

Abraham K. Korman

Baruch College--City University of New York

New York, NY

What Was Said

In commenting on the papers by Nieva and Tenopyr I find myself, in a sense, somewhat conflicted. On the one hand, there is almost nothing in these papers that I can argue with or that I can even question. Both authors have highlighted and stressed some significant issues that we all need to be concerned with. Nieva's highlighting of the problems associated with the two-career family, and the difficulty of being a single parent in terms of career implications, should particularly be noted. We have, of course, seen considerable concern in recent years with the former group but comparatively little that I know of with regard to the latter. It is time that we started to think about work implications of being a single parent. I am delighted to see this issue confronted.

I am also pleased to see Mary Tenopyr, a past president of the Division of Industrial and Organizational Psychology of the American Psychological Association, cite the impact of economic (i.e., inflation) and technological variables on human affairs. These variables are real, they are important and they do influence how we think, how we feel, and what we do. While I am not sure that I agree with all of her discussion (e.g., I think that changes in our aspiration levels may moderate and perhaps eventually decrease inflation), I am glad to see that she has brought up these matters to help us generate a wider range of testable hypotheses to work with.

What Was Not Said

Yet I must confess that that I do have some problems with both these papers for what they did not say. I also, perhaps, have some

problems with the general logic underlying what I see as the major
thrusts of our contemporary concerns with female labor-market participation. Let me be more specific.

In both of the papers, by Nieva and by Tenopyr, I see an underlying assumption that women = women; that black women = middle-class
women = white women = Hispanic women, etc. In fact, I see the same
assumption underlying much of our research and policy in this field.
Is this a reasonable assumption? I think not; no more than the
assumption that black men = middle-class men = white men = Hispanic
men. In some situations, perhaps, the assumption is an adequate
one; but certainly not in many others. After all, millions of women
at the lower end of the economic scale held full-time jobs for many
years before the impact of recent societal changes caught our attention. For them, as much as for their husbands, needs for income in
order to survive were and still are much more important than the
needs we hear expressed today from women with higher-level needs and
backgrounds. I mean not to deprecate either group but only to plead
for recognition of diversity among women as well as men and for the
use of adjectival qualifiers when appropriate.

A second lack in these papers, and perhaps also in the field at
large, concerns the continuing tendency to talk about female labor-
market participation and the relevant cultural factors involved
without talking about male labor-market participation and the relevant cultural factors involved there. How can one talk about one
group apart from the other? After all, males could not have done
the things they have done career-wise, both positive and negative,
without the coerced or non-coerced assent of women. We are all in
this together, men and women, and changes in one group affect
changes in the other group. I do not believe that it is possible to
understand or predict what will happen to women unless we also
understand what will happen to men, and vice versa.

My third concern has perhaps a somewhat broader base in a societal sense. Let me begin by first stating that I believe strongly
that we need to increase the ability of women to achieve their work
potential. To this end, we need to focus on organizational and
social sources of discrimination, the possible internal motivational
problems of women in attaining their work goals, and on ways in
which we can help women and men meet their child-bearing responsibilities while women attain their work goals. Our focus on work
goals for men and women, organizational productivity, personal job
satisfaction and, presumably (but not always), life satisfaction are
laudable goals, all of them; they are to be defended strongly and
not be apologized for at all.

Work-Family Conflict: The Major Question

What is my problem then? It may be briefly summarized. I
believe that the work-family conflict is the major question of our

time, and that positive outcome in one area relates to negative outcome in the other. I also believe that we, as a society, are
rapidly losing interest in the latter, i.e., in matters of human affiliation and social cohesiveness and that we as I-O psychologists
are contributing to this by disproportionate emphasis on work goals.
In additions, I believe that if we, as I-O psychologists, as well as
others, do not begin paying attention to these matters from the
viewpoint of saving and/or helping both institutions, the world of
the 1990's will be in such affiliative chaos that our current projections about labor force participation for men and women will be
largely out of whack. Let me expand on each of the above.

Nieva and Tenopyr both reflect on my first point but, I believe,
indirectly. I think we need to face up this issue more squarely.
There is a conflict, at least sometimes, as my students and I and
others have found consistently. We as I-O psychologists have to
face up to the fact that if we sometimes help work careers and organizations, we may also be hurting family life. The development
and/or recommendation of mobility plans for executives may be good
for an organization and for the career of the individual but it can
lead to the break-up of his/her family. In our studies we are consistently finding loss of affiliative satisfactions to be one of the
major causes of alienation among executives and managers. At one
level we can, of course, say that this is no concern of ours as I-O
psychologists, but I seriously doubt that many of us would adopt
this position. I say this not only in a humanistic sense but also
because the alienated manager, as we are also finding, is not a very
effective individual to have in an organization.

Will women, as they become executives and managers, also feel
this loss? I think so and our studies show this. Women do feel
this loss and it is not compensated for by the money they are
making. Our studies show that the correlation between income and
alienation is essentially zero.

Reconciling the Conflict

Can we reconcile this conflict? I think so. I think that we
must and that we have shown some increasing societal concern with
this conflict. I think we need to give it more attention if we are
to survive as a society; but this can only be done if we broaden our
scope beyond thinking only of how we can help women satisfy their
career and achievement needs. This is a laudable, desirable goal.
We need to attain it. However, it cannot be our only goal as a
society and as I-O psychologists. In Table 1 I have provided examples of some of the trends I see both in our society in general, and
in our organizations in particular, which are contributing, both intentionally and unintentionally, to a loss of affiliation concerns
in our society. In commenting on these trends, I should like to
make the following points:

Table 1.   Societal Factors (Including Organizational Factors)
           Influencing Deterioration of Human Affiliation

---

1.   Hypocrisy and Power--Materialistic orientation of
     Affiliative Institutions (e.g., Religious Institutions,
     Social Welfare Organizations)
2.   Degradation of "Flower Children" and "Hippie" Ethic
3.   Pornography and "Performance Orientation" of Contemporary
     Sexuality
4.   Contemporary (Over) Emphasis on Self-actualization
5.   Inherent Conflicts between Achievement and Affiliation in
     an Achievement-oriented society (e.g., the "Career
     Success/Personal Failure" Syndrome)
6.   The Bureaucratization of Society
7.   Growth of "Burn-out"--Growing Acceptance of "Burn-out" in
     People-oriented fields and our Unwillingness as a society
     To Do Anything About It
8.   Growth of and Social Support for "Workaholism"
9.   Hypocrisy of Male-Dominated Institutions--which say that
     they Value Affiliation but Do Not Support It
10. Tendency of Males to Reject Affiliative Needs until
     Mid-life
11. Decreasing Interest in Education and Social Concerns
12. Societal Acceptance of Divorce
13. Continued Acceptance and Support for the "Linear Society"
     (i.e., the use of economic and technological growth
     variables as criteria for societal success)
14. Societal and Media Manipulation of Affiliative Needs
15. Real Problems of Long-lasting Relationships
16. Increasing Societal Degradation of Parental Roles and/or
     Children

---

1.   The trends I have listed are neither
     inclusive nor complete--they are in
     a state of flux.
2.   In making my concerns evident here I
     wish in no way to deprecate the need
     for overcoming the implicit and
     explicit barriers that have blocked
     women's right to self-growth and
     self-development in the areas of
     career and vocational growth.
3.   The trends I have listed are
     apolitical in content and in thrust;
     I believe that organizations and
     societies cannot exist in the
     long-run without concern for
     affiliative need satisfaction,

particularly when we consider the
ties between organizations and the
world outside. I believe that this
is a reality which we all need to
recognize.

4. My reason for bringing these matters
up do not come from a desire to be a
"doomsayer." It comes from a desire
to point to a reality which we
should not ignore.

My last point is that we, as I-O psychologists, have a role to
play here. But what? I think that the role I see has been indicated by the foregoing comments. We need to expand our horizons
concerning our dependent variables. Achievement in a vocational
sense is not the only thing in life. It is a desirable goal which
we need to encourage but we need to be sensitive to what else we are
encouraging when we are encouraging work achievement. When we see
contradictions and negative outcomes we need to be concerned with
and seek out ways for reconciling the problems. We need to develop
and encourage alternate types of careers and lives and help to
change societal and organizational norms so that different alternatives are truly accepted and valued rather than merely tolerated.
Achievement motivation and achievement satisfaction are not an un-
mixed blessing for individuals, men or women, and we need to be sensitive to this in our thinking and in our research and our recommendations to the organizations that employ them.

PART III

LABOR AND MANAGEMENT IN THE '90's

HUMAN RESOURCE PLANNING AND THE INTUITIVE MANAGER:

MODELS FOR THE 1990's

James H. Reynierse

Virginia National Bank

Norfolk, VA

In my presentation I have three primary objectives. First, I will be making some futurist comments about the 1990's. I have taken the time frame of this conference quite loosely. As such, some of these trends may develop by the mid or late 1980's while others will appear in the 1990's. Secondly, as a strategic response to these trends, many organizations are developing corporate human resource planning functions. In this regard, I introduce a conceptual model of human resource planning emphasizing the practitioner's viewpoint. Finally, I introduce the methodological concerns of polythetic analysis, generalize to human resource planning and industrial-organizational psychology, and suggest that this is an appropriate methodology for examining "soft data" more rigorously.

The Environment of the 1990's

There are a number of trends which will significantly impact management in the future. For the most part middle managers with experience have been scarce and organizations have competed aggressively for this talent. This will change, perhaps within the current decade, and by the 1990's there should be an abundance or even glut of potential middle managers with many highly qualified individuals competing for scarce positions. The war babies born immediately after World War II will come of age and will be at a prime management age. In addition, many older managers will elect to delay retirement, either because legislation no longer makes retirement at 65 mandatory or due to economic necessity in which continued high inflation and the possible failure of our social security system makes retirement a luxury which few can afford. Finally, increased participation by women managers in the work force will only aggravate the problem.

At the same time and as a function of the same changing population demographics in which declining birth rates and a generally
aging population are primary contributors, we can expect a shrinking
supply of entry level workers. Historically industry has usually
taken for granted the availability of such a supply. In the future
such neglect will be unsatisfactory and creative employment practices will be necessary to successfully compete with other employers
and adequately staff organizations at hourly, nonsupervisory levels.
We can expect higher wages as one response to the scarce human resources at this level. Similarly, continued technological advances,
particularly in information processing areas, may produce a corresponding compression of functional responsibilities, particularly in
white collar industries. Thus, hourly clerical employees will routinely interface with computers, have access to more information,
and will have the discretionary responsibility that goes with this
access. In contrast, junior managers may lose their discretionary
responsibility to computerization. Finally, industry will become
increasingly capital intensive and shift from its current labor intensive orientation. For example, the development of electronic
funds transfer (EFT) systems in banking reflects both technological
advances and a response to the pressure of a labor intensive industry. EFT will be a common banking practice in the 1990's as will
the use of industrial robots in blue collar industries.

Another emerging trend is for employees to embrace an increasing
diversity of values both at work and at leisure. The new breed of
employee frequently challenges previously accepted institutions and
may sacrifice organizational commitment for a personally preferred
life style. The growing incidence of dual-career families makes re-
location economically and psychologically costly. How organizations
manage dual-career families may well become a primary focus of equal
employment opportunity and affirmative action during the 1990's.
These same values, perhaps amplified by high expectations, will
clash with the realities of population demographics. Thus, a
highly-educated work force desiring meaningful managerial work will
be increasingly frustrated on the job when few opportunities open
up. The satisfaction from accomplishment and meaningful work may
have to occur off the job through leisure time activities. With
frustration always ready to appear, it will become essential for
organizations to focus on the human resource needs of their
employees. Human resource issues will have to be addressed directly
and successful organizations will integrate their strategic and
operational plans with the needs and plans of their employees. As
such, there will be a premium on interpersonal skills throughout an
organization's supervisory and management group. While increasing
technological advances may increase the pressures for technically
knowledgeable and qualified managers, technical managers will have
problems if they are not just as effective in dealing with their
people.

Finally, and this may be my most controversial and speculative comment, I see the emergence of a paradox. On the one hand, our economic advantage will shift from heavy manufacturing industries, e.g., the automobile industry, to high technology information processing industries with a corresponding capability to handle "hard data" routinely. On the other hand, pressures to increase productivity through focusing on human resource considerations and to return to a more "human scale" will increase the value of "soft data". The impact on management will be a shift from that of a rational manager to a more intuitive, judgmental manager. At the bottom of this, I anticipate significant cultural changes as Western civilization and management practices move toward a more Far Eastern, Japanese management style.

What are some of the characteristics of the intuitive manager? Some terms which differentiate the rational manager from the intuitive manager are summarized in Table 1. One word of clarification is needed. While the rational manager is one polar extreme and the intuitive manager is another, this does not imply that the intuitive manager is irrational. Rather, the intuitive manager considers other realms (conditions) while are valued as just as important.

Although our culture emphasizes the rational side of man, there are several recent indications that an intuitive approach is becom-

Table 1. Comparison of the Rational and Intuitive Manager

Rational Manager	Intuitive Manager
Quantitative	Qualitative
Structured	Unstructured
Analysis, Reason, Logic	Intuitive
Certainty	Uncertainty
Status Quo	Change
Science	Art
Simplified (overly)	Complex
Figure (Gestalt)	Ground (Gestalt)
Rigid, Fixed	Flexible, Adaptive
Aristotelian (A or B), Occidental, Greek	Yin - Yang (A and B), Oriental, Chinese
Sensation	Perception
Corporate	Entrepreneurial
Hard	Soft

ing appreciated. Particularly noteworthy are several recent books,
all of which incorporate an intuitive component. Hofstadter (1979),
in Godel, Escher, Bach: An Eternal Golden Braid has written a particularly ecletic book which is destined to become a classic. The
correspondence of intuitive and formal approaches is a reoccuring
theme. A quite different approach is taken by both Maidment (1976)
in Robert's Rules of Disorder and Siu (1980) in The Master Manager.
Both are broadly intuitive and ultimately rely on quotations, para-
bles and folklore as they develop guidelines for effective management. Finally, Hamner (1980) has edited a book of readings entitled
Organizational Shock in which each selection comes from a non-traditional source but shows remarkable insight about how complex organizations function. I would add that the track record of artists and
authors in general, as well as the wisdom expressed in the proverbs
of many countries, is a legitimate reference and source of material
for the practitioner.

Unfortunately, Psychology as a discipline has been preoccupied
with its status as a science. Perhaps because of a collective in-
feriority complex, it has ignored complex and contradictory phenomena, denying the intuitive. Nevertheless, I suspect this idea has
been around all along but has not been fashionable. Psychology
needs a theory of intuition if it is going to seriously address the
complexities of human behavior. Some of the concepts from traditional psychology which may contribute to a better understanding of
the intuitive include figure-ground relationships and subliminal
perception from the psychology of perception. In learning psychology, the notion of incidental learning may be important. Within
clinical psychology, Reik's (1950) Listening with the Third Ear
suggests the need for a more wholistic and intuitive sensitivity.
Similarly, Isabelle Briggs Myers (1962), influenced by Jung, developed the Myers-Briggs Types Indicator in which intuitives are a
basic personality type. In industrial-organizational psychology,
assessment centers have been widely used and almost universally use
a sensitivity dimension for identifying potential managers and
supervisors.

A Conceptual Model of Human Resource Planning

In order to establish what I mean by Human Resource Planning
(HRP), let us begin by examining the term itself.[1] Human minimizes
the sexist implication of manpower. For the most part, however, the
phrase human resource planning is interchangeable with that of manpower planning. Resource emphasizes personnel as a basic corporate
resource. Just like buildings, equipment and physical inventories,
personnel are assets of any company. Planning emphasizes planning
as a management tool for implementing corporate priorities and solving corporate problems. Here, strategic planning and other forms of
intermediate and long range planning require that personnel requirements be addressed and that appropriate action plans be made.

Walker (1980) defines human resource planning as "the process of analyzing an organizations's human resource needs under changing conditions and developing the activities necessary to satisfy these needs". Taking a somewhat different point of departure, Hestwood and Biswas (1979) define it as "the process by which an organization anticipates the future human resource requirements of the organization and develops and implements policies and programs to fulfill those requirements". The interventions and programs of human resource planning should facilitate an organization's adjustment to change in its environment. Only by being responsive to these pressures can organizations continue to be successful and competitive.

As a response to the demographic trends and anticipated pressures outlined at the beginning of this paper, I developed a conceptual model of human resource planning for use within Virginia National Bank. The primary purpose of that model was to integrate the objectives, or needs, of the corporation with those of our employees.

Keep in mind that this is a model, not a formal system. As such it does not pretend to identify cause and effect relationships. Nor is there the requirement that the model correspond to some aspect of the real world. Still, such models are useful. From a practical point of view they are helpful in communicating human resource objectives and plans. This can be particularly valuable with line managers who have other priorities and are not intrinsically interested in human resource issues. Similarly, models may be useful in planning, identifying or prioritizing actions which the human resource practitioner may take. Finally, models may have considerable heuristic value. Thus, they may suggest gaps in existing programs for the practitioner while at the same time suggesting fruitful areas of data collection for the researcher. Conceptual models in human resource planning have been discussed previously by Milkovich and Mahoney (1978), and by Frantzreb (1979).

Figure 1 summarizes the primary components of the model. A skills analysis or other form of functional job analysis is the central process upon which all other human resource activities are ultimately dependent. While the model provides for additional inputs throughout the human resource planning process, a skills analysis is both a necessary condition and the starting point for further analysis and planning.

There are two additional central processes which are dependent upon an available skills analysis. On one hand, needs analysis represents a broad set of evaluation procedures for examining the existing status of organizations and individuals. On the other hand, potential analysis represents a broad set of procedures for determining the probability that someone will succeed in the future, provided the necessary developmental steps are taken. Thus, while

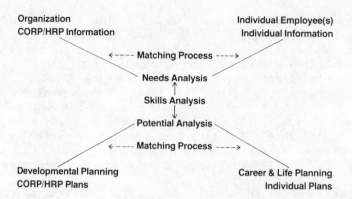

Figure 1.   The HRP Conceptual Model Integrating the Needs of the
Organization with Those of Its Employees.

in practice the evaluation and developmental steps for potential may
frequently occur together, commonly as part of the performance
appraisal process, this model emphasizes that they are conceptually
independent.

From both an organizational and individual perspective, matching
processes are essential throughout the human resource planning process.   These can be formal, e.g., a computer search, or informal,
e.g., a conference between an employee and management.   The model
values open communications and clearly indicates that organizations
must provide for both the exchange of information and plans in order
to achieve the best fit between organizational and individual objectives.

On the organizational side of the model there are corporate information and plans.   Corporate HRP information includes the most
basic information about an organization, including its structure and
strategic goals.   Corporate HRP plans include the developmental
planning necessary to achieve these goals as well as the active
management of that organizations's human resources.   On the individual employee side of the model there are individual information and
plans.   Individual information includes all of the information an
organization maintains concerning its employees.   Ordinarily this
includes that information maintained in personnel files and in automated personnel systems.   Individual plans include the career and
life planning which employees do to achieve their real and ultimate
goals.

Within an organization the optimal solutions to human resource
problems may differ widely depending upon the organizational level
at which they occur.   Human resource planning strategies by organizational level are summarized in Table 2.   For illustrative purposes

Table 2. Human Resource Planning Strategies By Organizational Level

Level	Selection Method	Allocation Method	Developmental Plan
Worker	ABA Tests/Interviews	Job Posting	Training Dept./ Performance Appraisals
Supervisor	Assessment Center	Job Posting	Training Dept./ Performance Appraisals
Management Trainees Junior Officers	Psychological Testing	Officer Job Posting	Training and Dept./ Performance Appraisals
Middle Management	Divisional HRP Committee	Divisional HRP Committee	Divisional HRP Committee
Senior Management	Corporate HRP Committee	Corporate HRP Committee	Corporate HRP Committee
Top Management	--	--	--

there are six levels, although realistically some of the distinc-
tions will be blurred in many organizations. The first level is
non-supervisory employees and subsequent levels go through the
supervisory and management structure to top management. Three human
resource planning issues are systematically addressed, namely how
individuals are selected for jobs at a particular level (selection),
how talent is distributed within an organization (allocation) and
how talent is trained for future assignments (development).

Human resource strategies at Virginia National Bank have primarily been directed to non-supervisory workers, supervisors and
management trainees and junior officers. The strategies identified
in Table 2 have been gradually developed and introduced as part of
systematic human resource planning at these levels. We use the
banking industry selection tests developed by the American Banking
Association (ABA) to assist us in selecting individuals for entry
level bank jobs. But we use a supervisory Assessment Center for
supervisors and psychological tests where we want to insure that our
trainees have long range potential and are competitive with our successful junior managers. As part of our open communication practices and a way of allocating human resources we have a highly successful job posting program in which employees can "bid" for current
openings. A separate posting program is available for officers. At
Virginia National, developmental planning is the responsibility of
each employee. However, they can receive individual assistance

through their supervisor, manager or personnel officer. The Training Department has administrative responsibility for developing and coordinating internal and external training programs.

At higher levels within an organization the emphasis shifts from administrative programs to an active management process directed to succession planning and continuity of management throughout the company. Many companies have adopted Divisional Human Resource Planning and Corporate Human Resource Planning Committees at these levels. Succession to top management involves other, often political, considerations. Still, some large companies are forming Human Resource Planning Committees within their Board of Directors to plan for succession at this level.

The classification of human resource planning programs and activities are summarized in Tables 3 and 4. Table 3 summarizes those activities which are primarily related to the central processes. Table 4 summarizes those activities which are primarily related to the organization and individual employees.

The Methodology of Polythetic Analysis

The subject matter of psychology, management and human resource planning is often fuzzy, both for the practitioner and researcher. To pretend that it is not limits our effectiveness and distorts our understanding of complex phenomena. Uncritical applications of "hard" methodologies to "soft data" may often be inappropriate. How then can we analyze "soft data" more rigorously?

Obviously we are not going to answer this question today. Rather, I would like to take this opportunity to introduce the methodology of polythetic analysis as one way of examining the "soft data" and complex phenomena inherent within human resource planning and industrial-organizational psychology without sacrificing the appropriateness and richness of this data.

Table 3. Human Resource Planning Analytical Activities

Needs Analysis	Skills Analysis	Potential Analysis
Attitude Surveys	Methodology	Psychological Testing
(Climate N.A.)	Research	Assessment Centers
Forecasting	Skills	Performance Appraisal
(Macro N.A.)	Job Descriptions	Replacement Charting
Training Needs Analysis	Job Analysis	Succession Planning
(Micro N.A.)	Job Families	
Performance Appraisal	Career Paths	

Table 4. Classification of Human Resource Planning Activities By
Organization and Individual Employee

Organization	Individual Employee
Corporate Information	Individual Information
Strategic Goals	Personnel File
Operational Goals	Employee Personnel Record
Organizational Structure	Skills Inventory
- Current	Career Profile
- Projected	Supply Information
Mission Statements	Management Information
	System
Charters	- Applicant Flow
Annual Reports	- Turnover
EEO/AA Goals	- EEO Reports
Policies	
Procedures	
	Individual Career and Life
Corporate HRP Plans	Plans
Recruitment	Selection Feedback
Allocation	- Assessment Center
Management Development	- Psychological Testing
Training Programs	Outplacement
Succession Planning	Personal Counseling
Individual Action Plans	Career Planning
(Managed Pool)	Interest Tests
HRP Plans	Individual Action Plans
EEO/AA Plans	(Personal)

Polythetic analysis is an approach associated with recent view-
points in biological classification (Sokal and Sneath, 1963; Sokal,
1966) and later introduced to comparative psychology by Jensen 1967;
1970).[2] The former and older classification system was based on
Aristotelian principles and has been termed monothetic because
classification was based on one or a few key characteristics. In
contrast, the newer approach has been termed polythetic because
classification is based on natural groups in which many characteristics are considered. For example, man has been monothetically
defined as "the featherless biped which talks". Unfortunately, this
definition is both too inclusive and too exclusive. Thus, it is inadequate because it includes a shaved, trained parrot in the ranks
of man but excludes a one-legged, deaf-mute who has been tarred and
feathered. Obviously man is much more than this and a polythetic
definition would embrace the diversity of characters, both morpholo-
gical and behavioral, which determine the class.

Polythetic analysis confronts complex phenomena directly, first
of all by looking at naturally occurring phenomena and secondly by

emphasizing the need to examine multiple variables, dimensions and characters within these natural events. Research oriented psychologists have addressed some polythetic issues through their research methodology. Thus, the factorial experiment in traditional experimental psychology allows the manipulation of several independent variables simultaneously. Similarly, multivariate analysis emphasizes the measurement side and provides for the correlation of several dependent variables simultaneously. Ethological analysis emphasizes both the naturalistic environment as well as the simultaneous observation and recording of many behavioral variables. Although such ethological and polythetic analyses have been successfully applied both naturally and in the laboratory, these approaches have been largely limited to basic research. They can, however, just as easily be applied in the natural environments of human resource planning and industrial-organizational psychology. Indeed, it is in just such real situations where the environment is uncontrolled and the data are "soft" that the convergent results of polythetic analysis can take on significance for the practitioner and researcher alike.

The need for multiple inputs and data is explicit within the framework of polythetic analysis. From a practitioner's viewpoint, within human resource planning this has been recognized implicity. Thus, many HRP methodologies systematically provide for multiple input. For example, the use of assessment centers for selection purposes rely on several exercises, dimensions and raters to arrive at targeted selection recommendations. Delphi techniques and Objective Judgment Quotient (OJQ), a proprietary process of Wyvern Research Associates, both obtain group concensus through multiple inputs when a group is physically separated and unable to meet together. Succession planning frequently involves group discussion with the group reaching concensus based on the shared comments of each group member. Clearly, the practitioner is often polythetic already. My guess is that the intuitive manager is basically polythetic as well.

Footnotes

1. This discussion is largely adopted from Walker, 1980.
2. The discussion comparing polythetic ad monothetic analysis is largely adopted from Jensen 1967 and 1970 and the interested reader should consult these papers for further development of these ideas.

References

Frantzreb, Richard B. Conceptual models of manpower planning. Manpower Planning, 1979, 3(8).

Hamner, W. Clay Organizational shock. New York: John Wiley and Sons, 1980.

Hestwood, T. & Biswas, B. Human resource planning and compensation: A developing relationship. Paper presented at the National Conference of the American Compensation Association, San Francisco, October 4, 1979.

Hofstadter, Douglas R. Godel, Escher, Bach: An eternal golden braid. New York: Vintage Books, 1979.

Jensen, D. D. Polythetic operationism and the psychology of learning. In W. C. Corning and S. C. Ratner (Eds.), Chemistry of learning. New York: Plenum Press, 1967.

Jensen, D. C. Polythetic biopsychology: An alternative to behaviorism. In J. H. Reynierse (Ed.), Current Issues in Animal Learning. Lincoln: University of Nebraska Press, 1970.

Maidment, R. Robert's Rules of Disorder. Gretna, LA: Pelican Publishing Company, 1976.

Milkovich, G. T. & Mahoney, T. A. Human resource planning models: A perspective. Human Resource Planning, 1978, 1(1), 19-30.

Myers, I. B. The Myers-Briggs Type Indicator. Palo Alto: Consulting Psychologists Press, Inc., 1962.

Reik, T. Listening with the third ear. New York: Grove Press, 1956.

Siu, R. G. H. The master manager. New York: John Wiley and Sons, 1980.

Sokal, R. R. Numerical taxonomy. Scientific American, 1966, 215, 106.

Sokal, R. R. & Sneath, R. H. A. Principles of numerical taxonomy. San Francisco: W. H. Freeman, 1963.

Walker, J. W. Human Resource Planning. New York: McGraw-Hill Book Co., 1980.

THE SETTING AND THE REALITY FOR LABOR RELATIONS IN THE 90'S

E. Douglas Kuhns

International Association of Machinists & Aerospace Workers

Washington, D.C.

Changing patterns in organization of the economy

The appearance of labor relations in the decade of the 90's will
depend on a good deal more than simply the changing composition of
the laborforce. Indeed, the economic changes that are taking place
in the current decade could very well spell the end of labor relations as we have known them. Whether this happens or not could very
well depend on the extent to which we can continue to conduct economic activity under the pattern of organization we have developed to
this time. (I should add, parenthetically, that I use the expression -- "the pattern of organization we have developed to this time"
-- advisedly. It certainly cannot be called a microcosm of highly
competitive units -- 700 firms do 70 percent of the nation's
business. Advances in technology would ultimately have reduced many
industries to a few units, anyway. Economies of scale have been
more the pattern than the exception. Some of our largest economic
units are publicly supported monopolies; some are, indirectly,
solely supported by government; some, on the other hand, conceivably
have taken over part of the government. But, this is the pattern of
organization we have developed to this time.) The extent to which
we can continue to conduct economic activity as we do, is considerably related to the state of the economy achieved through this pattern of organization to date.

Oddly, perhaps, and somewhat contrary to popular supposition,
the state of that economy is not bad. True, we persistently, over
the last decade, have had a slightly increasing long term rate of
unemployment. Some of the unemployed have been sustained by a
developing sub-economy (that is the bane of the Internal Revenue
Service); some have been sustained by collectively-bargained supple-

mental unemployment benefit plans, termination benefits, early retirement benefit plans, and public welfare benefit systems. But,
all of this has supported the purchasing power of consumer expenditures among the components of aggregate demand.

More recently, in the course of the latter part of the last decade, we have had an alarming rate of inflation. But, some of this
has been offset by an unregulated system of "partial indexing". Our
principal public transfer payments (social security, federal service
retirement payments, veterans benefits, unemployment compensation,
and workers compensation) have been wholly or partially indexed.
Producer oriented public utility and public service enterprise regulation has managed fairly immediate indexing through prescribed
rates of return (although, peculiarly, under an implicit assumption
of everlasting inelasticity of all demand curves involved). And the
computerized projections of future revenue requirements of the large
private corporations, factoring in as they do the necessary payments
of income taxes, the increase in employee compensation from the next
collective bargaining agreement, as well as the increase in energy
costs and even an assumption on the next year's inflation factor,
certainly manage their own indexing (albeit, again, under an implicit assumption of inelasticity of demand for their products, at
least upwards -- no one has considered the "down" side of a demand
curve lately, except American Motors). I hasten to add that collective bargaining is its own system of partial indexing.

All of this, of course, is not to say that we don't have some
serious problems. But, they are mostly "other peoples" problems.
They concern that part of the population that the economy could very
well get along without -- except that they won't go away. And, now,
the "problem" is getting a little more critical.

The general organization of the economy, somewhat ambivalently
described above, has brought us to a relatively high level of economic attainment. Until about ten years ago, we had the highest level
of real income in the world. Although, more recently, a number of
European countries and Japan now rival or have surpassed us, some of
this has been the result of some of our multi-national corporations
operating on an international profit margin, where rates of productivity overseas have been heretofore less exploited and relatively
higher. Meanwhile, our rate of increase in productivity, especially
with a considerable amount of technology being shipped overseas, has
decreased, and revitalization of some our own technology has been
sacrificed for the sake of the profit margin overseas.

Nevertheless, some rate of growth has continued. I note in particular the recent newspaper article commenting on consumer economist Sandra Shaber's observation that per capita real income has
increased 70 percent since 1960. Even the business cycle has not
been completely unkind. As a result of a considerable change in the

total organization of the economy, largely inadvertent, coming out of the depression and World War II in the decade between 1935 and 1945, we have not again had a major depression. This may startle some of you here, but I point out that all of our so-called recessions since have been part of three- or four-year cycles (traditionally called the Kitchin cycle) and have not been longer term major trade cycles (the Juglar cycle), such as that of the Thirties. This includes even the severe recession of 1974-75. One of the characteristics of such minor cycle recessions is that our great corporations have never "lost heart". Some of their decline in profit margins during such periods was a result of expansion in their investment and, consequently, their net worths, even while current revenues were falling off -- reflecting their long-run confidence in a constantly reviving economy.

But, the unemployment of the '74-'75 recession was more severe. The part of the economy we don't need got a little large. The political foundations were shaken some. An anonymous executive, quoted in Forbes magazine, confessed his view that if it had not been for SUB(Supplemental Unemployment Benefits) -- a collectively bargained benefit in a number of industries -- unemployment compensation and welfare, that period would have seen "people in the streets".

Now, with the changing composition of the population, that part of the economy is increasingly composed of older people, women, the young workforce and, particularly, young blacks. (Although there are some, I'm sure, who, feeling that the latter group is by far the more dangerous, believe that if we can just provide a few more prisons rather than welfare, we can take the "head" off that problem, too.)

The major problem that appears to have, within a relatively short period of time, brought the situation of the economy to "critical" is, of course, the energy problem. But, while it may have exacerbated the total situation, there are a number of other socioeconomic factors, some closely related, that have joined forces with the energy problem to produce within a relatively short period of time a situation which can be viewed as "critical", or at least, ominous.

In the early part of this century in a short paper evaluating, as he saw it, the state of theoretical economics, an English economist, Lionel Robbins, provided an important foundation for what came to be known as welfare economics -- a somewhat short-lived view of economic analysis, having little to do with the economics of the welfare state, or any other. Entitled as it was, "Those Empty Boxes", the article was directed towards identification of items of "cost" that were not evaluated in the neo-classical economic analysis of the traditional market system. In doing so, he merely anticipated a number of vexing problems that have come to pass. One of

his items that was not priced in the market system was the classic
case of smoke nuisance, which now has proliferated into a whole host
of "pollution" problems. He did not anticipate that a beneficient
democratic state would enforce pricing of these and other "hidden"
costs upon private enterprise. He merely wondered how wrong the
market system's allocation of resources was for not being able to
take account of such hidden costs.

Well, we have now found a way -- we have legislated the covering
of costs for anti-pollution measures, replenishment and recovery of
exploited resources, preservation of the environment, security and
safety of labor resources, and inclusion of costs for (avoidance of)
discrimination in the use of labor resources. We even now have some
partial costing incident to the "using up" of those labor resources,
in the deferred payments of pensions. Efforts are now being made to
evaluate the "diseconomies" involved in the waste of plant, resources and human resources connected with plant closings and
changes in location.

In the midst of all of this, no one has suggested that such
costs are not real. But no one wants to pay for them. The system
of private property ownership and the operation of the market system
are not organized to deal with them; so society, through the political system, is rapidly filling those empty boxes and attempting to
place the costs where they belong.

The changing composition of the population, and therefore, the
work force, has aggrevated many of these problems in fairly obvious
ways. We have an overgrown school system -- public and private --
that was overbuilt to handle the "baby bulge". However, not enough
of them were adequately trained for today's labor market, and while
many of the schools are empty, we now do not have enough nursing
homes for the aged, nor prisons for the "delinquents" who can't find
jobs.

And, on top of this comes the energy crisis. Right now, many of
us can afford to pay more for gasoline. But, the economy as a
whole, now appears to be figuratively "running out of gas".

The course of the last three or four cycles has been characterized by sluggishness in the recovery periods. Investment expendi-
ture, always regarded as the prime mover .in our style of economy,
has been particularly reticent. Profit margins have been less
attractive, new technology has been held back and productivity improvement has slipped. Government and consumer expenditures have
filled in the slack. An interesting by-product of this combination
has been a reduction in the amplitude of the cycle (with the exception of the drastic recession in 1974). The lagging participation
of investment has made the cycle less volatile. But, in the meanwhile, we have very little real growth.

In the short-run, we can reduce government expenditures and
taxes and inflation, ignore the "empty boxes" and stimulate investment and growth -- if consumer expenditures somehow sustain
themselves in the meantime, and the inducements for frozen capital
become sufficiently large. (Otherwise, the baby will go down the
drain with the bathwater.)

But, whatever the outcome of such short-term experimentation,
when the effort is at an end, the energy crunch will still be there
and the economy still will be faced by all of those "empty boxes",
which will further proliferate in the meantime.

Almost of equal consequence to the change in the composition of
the population is the dispersion of that population. At the present
time, 50 percent of the population is concentrated into three main
corridors in the country -- the Boston-Washington northeast
corridor, the Chicago-Cleveland lake corridor, and the San
Francisco-Los Angeles coast corridor. The ultimate consequences of
this have hardly unfolded.

The collapse of Detroit is imminent even if we kept out all
Japanese imports. Chrysler will not make it after four years (unless the Government should choose to go into business); Ford and
General Motors cannot be induced to build a car that can get sixty
miles to the gallon -- they might last too long. The consequent effect of Detroit's collapse on the steel industry boggles the mind.
The lake's corridor can become a shambles.

At one end of the coast corridor, Los Angeles has no rapid tran-
sit system. If the price of gasoline should go to $3 or $4 a gallon, Los Angeles might lose its pollution problem -- the entire area
might come to a grinding halt.

The northern end of the northeast corridor is in the more gra-
dual process of converting its cities from industrial to financial
centers, as its industrial components have sought to escape to the
sun-belt and a hopefully union-free environment.

Changing patterns in labor relations

Now, you ask me what are labor relations likely to look like in
the 1990's!

In this perspective, the outlook for the immediate future -- and
I mean the next two or three administrations -- is likely to be one
of agonizing reappraisal. The long-run problem of our style of
economy is whether or not our unused capacity and our less
accessible resources can be put into operation at full employment
levels of use if the prices of energy resources are going to make
otherwise profitable enterprise no longer sufficiently profitable.

In these circumstances, it makes little difference that there are vast, untapped reserves of coal, oil and gas under Antarctica, the Pacific Ocean, or elsewhere.

The beginning of what may happen to labor relations in such a long-run may be appearing in the auto industry. Here, in one company, there has been a tri-partite series of negotiations involving readjustment of terms and conditions of employment, terms and conditions of loans, and not too much adjustment of methods and the end products of production. The initial results have not been impressive. While the previous administration was reluctant to bail Chrysler out, it seems more certain that the current administration cannot, ideologically, "save" them. I visualize the production of automobiles currently taking place in this country as becoming quite unprofitable over the next few years. What is going to happen with that industry does not appear to be clear at all at this time. I cannot imagine the present administration undertaking the production of automobiles, nor even underwriting the losses of the industry.

The consequent effects upon the steel, rubber and related industries are fairly obvious. The first subsequent crisis likely would be in steel. This, perhaps, would be the best first case. I can see this administration, or any administration, contemplating the collapse of the steel industry with a certain element of panic. Even though steel might have contributed as much to its own demise as has the auto industry, the effect upon other industries would be such that an administration would have to be suicidal to let "nature take its course." The repercussions of this would be such that a number of other industries would become almost immediately depressed. We would very soon have to have a minimal level of top economic planning in which government and (preferably) consumers would be involved.

The look of labor relations in such enterprises would depend first upon the institutional arrangements that were made -- depending upon whether or not a government agency was going to operate the enterprise, participate in its operation, or simply underwrite it.

As this scenario began to unfold, other institutional forms, both public and private, could be undertaken. The shape of some of these already can be described. ESOP's (Employee Stock Ownership Plans) and TRASOP's(Tax Reduction Act Ownership Plans) are possibilities. There already have been some notable successes with Employee Stock Ownership Plans. They have been useful in a number of cases in which firms with large work forces were going to be closed, or removed to alternative locations. These types of ownership could be expanded with government (local or federal) financial backing, or actual participation. Some form of duplication of the English Public Utility Trust also could be expected.

With the development of such enterprises, one could reasonably
expect that there would be some revision, even some reduction, of
the conventional labor-management adversarial relations. But, these
might be replaced by others. Depending upon how the institutions
were developed, there might be a considerable consumer representation, through direct government representation or otherwise. In
some cases, however, a separate government interest, apart from consumer interests, might be identifiable and have separate representation.

Adversary relations would certainly continue in some form over
negotiation of terms and conditions of work, although the combination of employment and ownership in some cases might modify the outcome. Consumer ownership and government representation, however,
would expand the types of adversary relations. As one writer has
suggested: "Since worker performance, remuneration and job tenure
are ultimately at issue, the parties should pursue worker participation and consultation on such important matters as the financial
plans of the enterprise, investments, plant design, markets, products and pricings." (Stephen Schlossberg, UAW)

There is no question that such extensive changes in the characteristics of the institutions involved in such negotiations will
change the subjects of bargaining. Changes in legislation will be
required. The role of government in the economy will increase
whether anybody likes it or not. The far-reaching changes beginning
to be apparent in the changing composition of the workforce will be
more adequately dealt with within such a broadening framework of
economic institutions.

In the first place, the currently developing pattern of population growth and its dispersion (or lack thereof) will have to be
dealt with as the energy crisis worsens. Resources, including labor
resources, are going to have to be brought together in new combinations and in new locations. New enterprises in the future are going
to have to have the parties involved, or in negotiation, deal with
the removal of labor resources from one area to another, the housing
of that labor when it cannot transport itself from home to work over
long distances, the care of children when their working parents are
at work, and the needs of both when they are not at work.

Our large urban areas may not be "doomed", but they are going to
be considerably "sliced" up. One can see some of this process beginning in some cities now. Certain urban areas within our largest
concentrations are never going to be rebuilt -- no one wants to be
there. Instead, satellite sub-urban areas are developing, sometimes
around industrial complexes; sometimes the industrial complex is
moved in afterwards.

Will all of this happen fast enough? And, will it be "profitable" enough? Probably not, unless there is some long-term financing and some extensive planning. Can private enterprise as it is now constituted, with its current requirements for profits and the present limitations of money markets, do this?

Consider a few items that trade unions have bargained over very little, or not at all. There have been a few cases in which we have bargained over the installation of company-related or company-maintained medical facilities, usually in isolated areas. But, this was less expensive than securing medical care any other way. We have a national policy, and the federal government has a national policy, favoring group practice medical care, because it is more effective and less expensive. We really have not begun to push this one yet.

There are a few cases where unions have bargained for employer payments to subsidize retirement homes for members. We have a few cases in which we have bargained for day-care centers. There are even a few cases in which payments, that otherwise could have been a part of wages, have been bargained into alcoholic and drug treatment centers. I can even recall a couple of cases, long before the days of the Environmental Protection Act, when a few cents-per-hour were bargained into anti-pollution devices because a couple of unions wanted a couple of rivers cleaned up for the kids.

We have bargained over apprenticeship and training. In our organization, we have a fair amount of this. But, generally, employers do not want to do this because it is expensive. Yet, we have constant complaints from our employers that there is a great shortage of skilled labor.

As the workforce becomes older, with an increasing proportion of women, retraining is going to have to be organized for more people. Is private enterprise willing to take this on? My current view, from some experience, is that we will never get this out of our presently constituted educational institutions.

We have done a great deal of bargaining over pensions. The combination of an increase in the proportion of older workers and the interest stimulated among younger workers by the recent requirement of ten-year vesting has raised this issue in collective bargaining to a level of importance probably secondary only to wages. Although all aspects of a pension plan are negotiable, virtually all employers categorically refuse to bargain method of liability computation, assumptions, amortization of past service, administration, or even the investment categories in which the workers' money is to be invested.

We have not bargained over the products to be produced -- we have not represented consumers. We probably should have. Three or four years ago, before Leonard Woodcock became Ambassador to China, he was asked by a TV commentator why the UAW had not used some of its enormous strength to demand that the industry make smaller, more efficient automobiles. In some horror, Woodcock was at some pains to explain that such a demand would have been a violation of managerial prerogatives and was not a subject for bargaining under the labor agreement.

But, these are digressions. The point simply is that: To the extent that the needs of low and moderate income people for transportation, other public services, safety, health, even education, cannot be provided through the, heretofore, more economic medium of the state, unions and other coalitions will increasingly look to the bargaining table as the only alternative source. Can private enterprise stand all of that?

I suppose it is conceivable that technology might bail us out once again. Many point to the fact that there is a great deal of highly sophisticated technology around that has not been harnessed to effective production yet. This is, of course, precisely the point -- it has not! Technology without investment is almost useless, and we have already indicated that it is investment that is "in drag".

There is hardly any question that this has been the instrument of our declining rate of productivity increase through the decade of the Seventies. Investment has lagged, new technology has not been brought into place, and productivity improvement slacked off. Over generations, improvement in technology has been responsible for most increases in productivity -- that, and discovery of new, cheap resources. (If you note that I do not relate productivity to output per man-hour, it really does not matter to me whether it is expressed that way or in "ergs", "ohms", or even "foot-pounds".)

But, as might be suggested, some of this sophisticated new technology is terribly expensive, even by present standards, and use of some of it involves commitment of investment over a long period of time before final payoff. Added to other dis-economies of "disinvestment" in many large-scale enterprises, these difficulties could spell out the demise of some of our older industries.

As a matter of fact, over the course of the last two cycles, there have been occasional citations, in the Wall Street Journal, and elsewhere, of cases of business enterprises expanding operations on the basis of a larger component of labor in relation to capital than was the case before. These were not cases in which the new capital investment was that much more efficient than the old; they were cases of substitution of labor for capital.

The potential implications of this kind of reversal are enormous, because it reverses the historical pattern of our economic development, one in which the relative expensiveness of labor, in relation to resources, was a constant incentive for technology and capital development as the path to profits.

Changing economic conditions, changing institutions, changing coalitions, expanded negotiations, more public participation, are going to set the stage for labor-relations in the '90's. As we temporize with current economic conditions, we may slip into these changing patterns gradually and gracefully, or things may get a great deal worse before they get better.

LEADERSHIP AND MANAGEMENT IN THE 1990's

Bernard M. Bass

State University of New York at Binghamton

Binghamton, NY

So many people including myself have speculated about management
and labor in the year 2000 (Bass, 1968, 1972, 1976; Bass &
Ryterband, 1973; Ryterband & Bass, 1973) that I thought it might be
useful today to focus in more detail on one important element
involved -- leadership. My motivation is also influenced by the
fact that I have just completed a revision of the Handbook of
Leadership (Stogdill & Bass, 1981). I noted there in a concluding
chapter on future research in leadership that we can look ahead in
several ways by extrapolation. We also can examine societal forces
that will shape organizational management in the 1990's. Finally
revolutionary paradigms may appear.

Trends

Straight-line extrapolation from current trends in leadership
practices, training, development, and research would lead us to expect that the topic itself will occupy even more attention than it
does today due to the increasing complexity of the human, technological and economic forces at work.

Societal trends have been discussed here already in detail.
About 1965, the majority of the U.S. force shifted from manufacturing to service. Opportunities to increase productivity increasingly
have come to depend on effective human relationships and the development of personnel. In the same way, the cost of labor relative to
total organizational output of goods and services continues to rise,
exacerbated by the sudden inflation in the cost of energy required
if humans are replaced with machines. Industrial democracy is
likely to become a fact of life in the U.S. as it is now in Western
Europe. The percentage of relations-oriented personnel in the U.S.

labor force has dramatically increased with the sharp increase in
the employment of women. A plural society of varied ethnicity and
race is replacing the ideal of assimilation. The multinational firm
with its world-wide outlook continues to expand. Foreign investment
in the U.S. has risen sharply as well.

We are likely to see leadership research continuing to reflect
these societal developments. Thus, Pascarella & Cook (1978) forecast that a premium will be placed on the middle managers' abilities
to deal with the human factor. And more statesmanship will be required of top managers.

Faced with the turnover and low quality problems of the all-
volunteer Armed Services, by 1990 we may see universal service
required of 18 and 19 year olds of both sexes. Again, attention may
be focused on new approaches to promoting stability and cohesiveness
through better leadership. Educational leadership in the 1980's is
also likely to take a sharp turn in the face of declining enrollments. A more energy-conserving world generates both the requirement for better relations as well as the mounting concerns for productivity. Needed will be more research on how these are best
merged. Increasingly, there will be less toleration of laissez-
faire leadership. But care will have to be exerted to avoid a drift
back to promoting autocratic behavior in the guise of active leadership, particularly if unemployment and job insecurity remains high.

The world of computerized management information systems, the
organization predicted over twenty years ago by Leavitt & Whistler
(1958) for the 1980's has arrived. We will be learning more about
managers' interactions with each other, with superiors, peers, subordinates and clients, that have been altered by computerization.

New Paradigms

As for new paradigms, we have already seen the rapid impact of
social learning theory. Uses for catastrophe theory from mathema-
tics may be found with much wider appreciation of natural discon-
tinuities in leader-follower relationships. The social science of
leadership may be impacted by new ways of looking at phenomena
developed in twentieth century physics. For example, a willingness
to accept two distinct ways for dealing with the same phenomena may
lead leadership theorists to treat simultaneously the leader's and
the subordinate's rationales and rationalizations for what is
happening. Cause-and-effect analyses may be seen as the exception
compared to mutual interactions.

We are likely to see more borrowing across countries of leadership and manaegment approaches with the ever-increasing internation-
alization of business. Don't be surprised if in the 1990's many
U.S. companies are using the Japanese Ringi method of full and

deliberate consultation. In the same way, Likert's overlapping
groups may be widely practiced in Japan by then.

Towards a New Task-Oriented Society

In 1960, in Leadership Psychology and Organizational Behavior
(Bass, 1960), I introduced a trichotomy for understanding why people
attempt to lead -- task, interaction and self-orientation.
Societies were seen to be characterized as being dominated by one of
these themes and possibly cycling from task-orientation (an era of
growth and development) to interaction-orientation (an era of conso-
lidation) to self-orientation (an era of conflict and decline). At
that time we were near the end (but didn't know it) of the Age of
Conformity. The major themes of the 1950's had been illustrated by
the Man in the Grey Flannel Suit and Riesmann's (1950) outer-
directedness. The consumer was king. Sensitivity training meant
learning how to be a good group member. Marketeers dominated U.S.
industry. Productivity kept rising at a 3 or 4 percent rate per
year. It was only a matter of being able to sell all that could be
produced. To me, we were then as a society more interaction-
oriented, focussing on maintaining good peer relations, staying in
line ourselves and enjoying each other's company. The peak matur-
ation of interaction-orientation was probably encapsulated in J. F.
Kennedy's: "Ask not what your country can do for you; ask what you
can do for your country." This was in contrast to the U.S. of an
earlier era where our heroes were the task-oriented producers; the
inventors, engineers and builders. Getting the job done was seen as
a good in its own right. In 1960, I suggested that the long task-
oriented, nation-building, Horatio Alger period in the United States
had given way to an emphasis on interaction-orientation and that
this in turn, in some far distant future, would give way as in India
to a third phase in the cycle -- self-orientation emphasizing self-
concerns, extrinsic rewards, loyalty to self, praise and ego needs.
Little did I know then how fast this turning inward would begin.
Haight-Ashbury was just around the corner. How do you imagine
Kennedy's inaugural admonition sounded in Vietnam in 1969?

But we now seem to be at a more mature phase of societal
self-orientation where books appear on the importance of organizational members recognizing their self-interests and acting constructively to further them (Culbert & McDonough, 1980). It is a
far cry from what was meant by being a good group member. Sensitivity training now focuses on increasing self-awareness and personal growth instead of group dynamics. Formal career planning for
the individual organizational member begins soon after entry if not
before joining the organization. Our heroes are now anti-heroes in
contrast to those in the era of growth. The leaders of industry are
accountants and lawyers, the experts in dealing with constraint and
regulation. Short-term investment strategies dominate the scene.

What about the 1990's? It is quite possible that the peaking
out of self-orientation will coincide with an end to the disloca-
tions, declining expectations and real standard of living due to
readjustment to a new world of high-priced energy. The adjustment
may be aided by the reappearance of task-orientation as the dominant
theme.

As this new era of growth and development appears, technically-
oriented knowledge workers will move to the top of organization
replacing lawyers and accountants of the 1970's and 80's and the
marketeers of the 1950's and 1960's. (General Electric has just
made this shift.) A new kind of work ethic may become popular with
the return of a prosperity of goods and services. However, new problems will appear in the new century. As relatively few people are
required for production, increasingly robotized, most jobs will be
in service, and there will probably be a considerable oversupply of
people to fill them. But as I predicted in 1974 (Bass, 1974), by
2000, we may have a new leisure class of "have-nots" subsidized by
the "haves". The "haves" will tend to be employed in challenging,
creative work. Much of the dull and routine will have been automated out of existence. Nevertheless, for those onorous dirty jobs
which cannot be fully automated, high pay and short working hours
will compensate.

LEADERSHIP AND MANAGEMENT DEVELOPMENT

More Accommodation to Individual Differences in Leader Personality

On the one hand, much of the current concern for contingencies
affecting leader-subordinate outcomes may be seen as a chimera in
the light of the demonstrated erroneousness of the law of small numbers. On the other hand, Fiedler (1977) may be right. More attention may be paid to the relatively unchangeable personality of the
leader who needs to be transferred to situations that fit his personality or to train leaders to adjust situations to better match
their personalities. Just as "one best way" gave way to situation-
alism, we may begin to emphasize differential optimum contingencies
for different leaders. Path analytic research by Farrow (1976) suggests that directive leadership is mainly the outcome of autocratic
leader personality rather than situational contingencies. Partici-
pative tendencies, on the other hand, depend on such situational
factors given less autocratic personalities as leaders.

Unfortunately, little research has been done so far on the interaction of power with leader behavior and personality. Questions
such as the following remain to be answered. Will a group respond
positively to a leader with high (or low) power who exhibits one of
the task-oriented patterns of behavior as opposed to a leader who
exhibits one of the person-oriented styles of behavior? If so, how

will the personality structure of the group members and the urgency of the group task affect the response? Are there patterns of leader personality that may mitigate in some degree the adverse effects of coercive and reward power? Will coercive power and strong control be more readily accepted under high rather than under low degrees of leader-follower value similarity? What factors tend to legitimize different forms of power among group members? What factors tend to legitimize different forms of power in the eyes of observers who are not members of the group?

Dyadic versus Group Relations

The dyadic approach can be applied with considerable utility. For example, sanctioning and punitive leader behavior seems to be the result rather than the cause of inadequate subordinate performance. Leaders have "A" lists and "B" lists of subordinates. The "A"'s are kept psychologically closer; "B"'s are kept psychologically more distant. Work-oriented leaders are likely to relegate the more incompetent of their subordinates to the "B" list, and to treat them more punitively. But the "A"'s will be expected to be more loyal and obedient and required to maintain higher standards of performance. Contrarily, person-oriented leaders may exert extra effort with their black sheep, seeing their most competent subordinates as sources of conflict by their deviation in performance to the upside of group norms. The linkages to Fiedler's LPC (least preferred co-worker) are apparent.

Focus on Perception

Considerable exploitation of attribution phenomena can be applied with profit to the leader-follower relationship. The leader's behavior toward subordinates appears to be strongly determined by the reasons -- ability, motivation, luck, or circumstance -- the leader gives for the subordinate's performance. In the same way, subordinate's attributions of the reasons for the leader's behavior will strongly relate to the subordinates' satisfaction. The leader judged by subordinates as willing but incompetent seems to be more forgivable than the leader judged competent but unwilling.

As we have already noted, conscious perceptions can seem to determine the leader's subsequent efforts. thus, Nebeker & Mitchell (1974) found that differences in leadership behavior could be explained by the leader's expectations that a certain style of leadership would be effective in a given situation. At the same time, subordinates' descriptions of their leaders' behavior may be distorted by their implicit theories about leadership, particularly where they lack real information about the situation and are inclined therefore to fall back on stereotypes (Schreisheim & deNisi, 1978).

For improving relationships, what we are likely to see developing is the idea of leaders and subordinates sharing their rationales and ideologies about influence processes.

Focus on Transformational Rather Than Transactional Leadership

In the military, in government, and in industry there are calls for more leaders and fewer officers, politicians or executives. Such persons are needed to show us how to master and motivate institutions and individuals within a complex environment experiencing excessive internal and external stresses and changes (Mueller, 1980).

Leaders need to learn more about how to move subordinates toward the acceptance of superordinate goals, how to arouse followers into self-transcendence, how to move a group from complacency, hasty responses, inertia or defensiveness in the face of threat to complete and adequate vigilance. If a group is primarily focused on its lower level safety and security needs, a leader needs to learn how to move it toward concern for recognition and achievement. If a group is under stress too high for coping with the complexity of the situation, the leader needs to know how to steady and calm the group.

We may be avoiding stressing the need for transformational leadership because when seen in the everyday manager, it is often merely autocratic, coercive behavior dressed up as charismatic (Culbert & McDonough, 1980). Publicly, subordinates fully comply; privately, they reject the leader and display all the side effects accruing from their leader's use of coercive power.

Managers, battalion commanders, teachers, coaches and directors can be found who fit the description of persons to whom followers form deep emotional attachments, and who in turn inspire their followers to transcend their own interests for superordinate goals, for goals higher in level than previously recognized by the followers. Even in hardened bureaucracies, there are leaders whose knowledge of the system is coupled with good connections; who have the ability to mobilize and husband resources, who keep their eyes on the bigger issues, and who take the risks required for "creative administration". This gives them the idiosyncracy credit to arouse in subordinates complete faith and trust in the leader and the willingness to strive for the higher goals set forth as challenges for the group by the leader.

The question is: Can we take what Burns (1978) saw primarily for transforming leadership at the mass level and apply the concept to the small group situation? Are there analogues in the small group for the intellectual leaders, reform, revolutionary and heroic leaders who transform societies? How can we obtain the benefits

without the associated costs of heroic leadership characterized by
followers' strong belief in the leaders as persons above and beyond
their competence? How can we gain the benefits without the costs
associated with strong faith that the leader will make it possible
for the group to succeed, resulting in willingness to give the
leader power to act in crises. Such a leader can inspire, legitimize, guide and enlarge the arena of action to manage conflicting
interests successfully. The result is a transformed followership
into something greater than before.

Robert K. Mueller (1980), Chairman of the Board of Arthur D.
Little, described "leading-edge" leadership. Such leadership deals
with "fuzzy futures". It is able to simplify problems and to jump
to the (correct) crux of complex matters while the rest of the crowd
is still trying to identify the problem. Mueller saw the need to
understand this "rapid reification". Second, he saw the need for
leadership integrating and relating a charismatic component with the
logical and intuitive attributes vital to leading-edge leadership.

Leaders as Organizational Politicians

The well-trained leader in the 1990's will be familiar with what
the social sciences have to say about organizational decisions emerging from coalitions, negotiations and other political processes.
Organizational decisions often can be understood as a consequence of
coalition formation and negotiations and other political processes.
Decisions are based on the relative power of those involved rather
than the merits of the issue. Culbert & McDonough (1980) see as a
challenge for leaders their effective brokering inside and outside
their own group. Inside, such brokering should try to negotiate
arrangements within their subordinate group that makes for the best
possible mix of subordinate's serving their own self-interests as
well as meeting the needs of the group. Externally, the leaders as
representatives can often do much to increase the group's resources
and opportunities through effective negotiations with outsiders and
superiors. While such negotiating behavior with individual
subordinates seems to be counterproductive as a leadership style,
playing the role of broker successfully with peers and superiors
still seems important to the successful manager.

OTHER TRENDS

New Patterns of Leadership

With the increase in the advancement of women, ethnics and
blacks into positions of leadership, we expect to see systematic
changes in effective leadership patterns. It is true that masculine
women (assertive, systematic, task-oriented, etc.) are likely to be
promoted into management. At the same time, women who are promoted,

and the most successful among them, are more masculine. Nevertheless, one can see the possibilities that with so many women moving
upward, new norms for managerial success will emerge in which some
of what we regard as more feminine may appear.

Organizational Trends

I will conclude with some additional predictions about organizational life that I made in 1967, 1973 and 1976, which I still see as
likely forecasts for the decades ahead generating newer forms of
leadership and influence processes:

--More managers interacting with a computer terminal than with
  another human

--More managers operating via cable or satellite from their
  homes rather than face-to-face

--Less traveling and more teleconferencing

--More stress due to information overload

--More industrial democracy--"federal and state legislated
  employee representation in management"

--More employee-owned firms

Currently, we are early in the Reagan administration and its
thrust to reverse or slow down the trends toward regulation and central planning in favor of a more laissez-faire position by the Federal government. I can't help but feel that by 1988 or 1992, partly
in reaction to what occurred in the 1980's, a coalition of environ-
mentalists, women's and minority rights groups, social activists,
educational interests, the older population, the anti-gun, and other
liberal forces will have won the mandate for a new political leadership which will have learned how to coalesce these diverse interests
into a majority vote. Such leadership will pick up the pieces of
OSHA, the EPA, CETA and so on, reduced and reformed during the 80's,
possibly incorporating much of the shift from central to state
government now in process. The result will be an expanded push into
new kinds of working relations and influence patterns among
industry, government and education guided by state and national
planning characteristic at present of Japan and the Continental
European countries.

References

Bass, B. M. Leadership, psychology and organizational behavior.
    New York: Harper and Row, 1960.

Bass, B. M.   Implications of behavioral sciences in the year 2000.
    Management 2000.   New York: American Foundation for Management
    Research, 1968.

Bass, B. M.   Organizational life in the 70's and beyond.   Personnel
    Psychology, 1972, 25, 19-30.

Bass, B. M. & Ryterband, E. C.   Work and organizational life in
    2001.   In Dunnette, M.D. (Ed.), Work and non-work in the year
    2001.   Monterey: Brooks-Cole, 1973.

Bass, B. M.   Self-managing systems, Z.E.G. and other unthinkables.
    In Meltzer, H. and Wickert, F. R. (Eds.), Humanizing organiza-
    tional behavior.   Springfield, Ill.:   C. C. Thomas, 1976.

Burns, J. M.   Leadership.   New York: Harper and Row, 1978.

Culbert, S. A. & McDonough, J. J.   The invisible war.   New York:
    John Wiley and Sons, 1980.

Farrow, D. L.   A path analytic approach to the study of contingent
    leader behavior.   Ph.D. Dissertation, University of Rochester,
    1976.

Fiedler, F. E.   The contingency model and the dynamics of the lea-
    dership process.   In L. Berkowitz (Ed.), Advances in experimen-
    tal social psychology, Vol. II.   New York: Academic Press,
    1978.

Leavitt, H. J. & Whistler, T. L.   Management in the 1980's.   Harvard
    Business Review, 1958, 36, 41-48.

Mueller, R. K.   Leading-edge leadership.   Human Systems Management,
    1980, 1, 17-27.

Nebeker, D. M. & Mitchell, T. R.   Leader behavior: an expectancy
    theory approach.   Organizational Behavior and Human Performance,
    1974, 11, 355-367.

Pascarella, P. & Cook, D. D., Can you win?   Industrial Week, 1978,
    196(2), 75-84.

Riesman, D.   The lonely crowd.   New Haven: Yale University Press,
    1950.

Ryterband, E. C. & Bass, B. M.   Perspectives in the context of
    change.   In Dunnette, M. D. (Ed.), Work and non-work in the
    year 2001.   Monterey: Brooks-Cole, 1973.

Schreisheim, C. A. & deNisi, A. S., The impact of implicit theories
    on the validity of questionnaires.   Unpublished manuscript,
    1978.

Stogdill, R. M., & Bass, B. M.   Handbook of leadership.   Revised
    Edition.   New York: Free Press, 1981.

REFLECTIONS ON POLARITIES AND BIAS

Clayton P. Alderfer

Yale University

New Haven, CT

I am a biased person. Occasionally, when I am with people who call themselves psychologists, I think saying that means I am not one of them. On the other hand, it is possible that I am not the only biased person in the world of psychology and that others, too, have biases. As a matter of fact, when I think not only of the part of the conference where this panel participates, but also take account of the sessions that preceded us, I believe that this conference, as a whole, is an example of how to use bias in the service of research in organizational psychology. Here are two examples of bias that have impressed me recently.

The first was stated by a former chairman of the board of a major corporation. He learned that I had done research on race relations in organizations. He was a bit older than he thought I was, and was feeling the effects of his age on my interest in race. After a brief exchange -- which was relatively descriptive, calm, and unshaped by emotionalism -- he looked at me "square in the eyes," as the saying goes, pointed his finger at me with some emotion, at least in the lower part of his arm, and said; "Young man, I want you to know that people never tell the truth about race in organizations."

I said, "How is that?" And he said, "A friend of mine, who runs a major corporation, recently told me that he had conformed in total to the rules of affirmative action, and thus had a 10% minority at every level in the organization. At the same time he had a 10% reduction in profits in his company." I did not ask him whether he was explicitly going to make the causal association; nor did I ask him whether he thought he was telling me the truth. I know of no organization that has 10% minority at every level in the organization and I doubt very seriously if anybody could make a causal connection between whatever percentage of minority people this fellow had in his organization at whatever level, and the phenomena, if it were true, that he had suffered a 10% decrease in profitability.

The second example was set off by the first panel in this program who talked about the subject of age. When I listened to the people, I instantly became uncertain as to what ageism is. I happen to be 40 years old, and for some folks that makes me old, and for others it makes me young. The ones for whom I am old are in their 20s or 30s. Those for whom I am young, like the executive I just spoke about, are usually at least in their late 40s, if not older. After I listen to the speakers, I got a little clearer. Ageism is not necessarily discrimination against older people, although it might be. For example, some of the younger panel members seemed to have a different interpretation of the data than Harold Sheppard. Just for the sake of making sure that we all do not decide too quickly what ageism is, I call attention to a book called Generations Apart (Shellec, 1981). Its theme has to do with prejudice of the old against the young. I might also point out to you that in large corporations there are not a vast number of people who are under 50 years old and in senior management positions.

I make one other reference to earlier panels. One of our earlier speakers made the statement, "We need to treat men as a group and then deal with age subgroups within that group of men." He was especially interested in men who were over 50 and who held senior positions in organizations. Now I think that is a very wise suggestion. It also helps me make the transition into the subject of the biases of my fellow speakers on this panel.

I want to identify the primary biases unstated by each of the speakers. Let me start with Jim Reynierse. I think his notion is that the function of behavioral science is to control the middle of the organization more effectively. If I move to Doug Kuhns; his bias, I think, is that the behavior of labor is primarily an economic phenomenon, and we do not need to think too deeply about this behavioral, psychological stuff. And then moving to Bernie Bass: it seems to me, he thinks of leadership as primarily a management function. For example, he does not, or did not, say much about the leadership of labor and how that shapes and will shape the future of organizational psychology in the 1990s.

Identity groups and organization groups

To make my biases also clear, to the extent that I am able, I would like to let you know that I come to this role of discussant as somebody who has a set of theoretical constructs for understanding organizations and, therefore, the biases that derive from those concepts. An important distinction is that between what I call identity groups -- which are the groups that people belong to as the function of their ethnicity, their gender, their age, and their families; and the organization groups -- that people belong to as a function of the place and position they occupy in a given organization at some point in time.

Identity groups are things that are biologically determined. Biology tells us about our ethnicity, about our family, about our age, and about our gender. There is either no change in those conditions or very slow change, such as that which occurs as a function of the life cycle. Given the marvels of modern medicine, there are some who are also able to undergo a gender change by surgical intervention. Organization groups, on the other hand, are far more temporary and more subject to the whims of the people around us who are in the organization; particularly those who hold power. One of the underlying themes of this conference is that organization groups are not independent of identity groups.

Perhaps older people face a kind of hard reality; that they are either in charge, or that they are relegated to relatively obscure or non-existent positions. We all also know that the number of minority people who exercise significant positions of influence in the largest corporations in the United States is not vast, to say the least. We can see that indirectly, simply by observing the membership of this conference.

These facts have some interesting implications for organizational psychology. It is possible to stop thinking of variables like age, race, and sex as "individual difference variables." It is possible to think more in terms of each of us as a group representative. This means that we represent not only our organization groups, such as that level in the hierarchy or that department we come from, but also our identity groups. I stand here before you as a white, 40-year old male, who also is a professor at Yale University, in the School of Management. I believe that it is very difficult for many of you, whether you are conscious of it or not, to take account of me without being influenced by those variables. Some may play a heavier part than others. For instance, if you also happen to be a white male, you will probably respond more to the Yale University and the professor part of those group identities. If you happen not to be a white male, my guess is you respond more to the white and male, and eventually to the 40-year old part, then you do to the Yale University and professor. This is simply to illustrate the way in which one thinks if he or she uses what I call an intergroup perspective to understand behavior in organizations.

The intergroup perspective is useful, not only in understanding the intergroup dynamics of an organization, but also in understanding the individual behavior of members and the life of small groups in organizations. One of the things that people, I think, tend to over-

look is that group behavior is not just something that grows inside
of groups. The life of a group has external manifestations and, in
turn, those external manifestations show up in the life of the group.
For example, it seemed to me quite productive and fruitful that our
panel on male-female dynamics included men and women. My guess is
that if that had not been the case, the points of view that we have
heard might have been quite different. Similarly, the panel on age,
while not as explicit in identifying themselves by age, nonetheless
showed differences in theory and interpretation of data that struck
me as notably related to the ages of the speakers.

Turning to the present panel, we find similar philosophies occurring in terms of organization groups. Jim Reynierse, as a manager,
speaks a management's point of view, or at least middle-management's
point of view. Doug Kuhns, as a representative of organized labor,
speaks a labor perspective. And Bernie Bass, who is at the high end
of the pyramid in the academic world, speaks of leadership from primarily a managerial perspective. I think it is useful to remember
that none of us, and this includes me -- although given my special
insights I might escape the problem -- none of us, really escapes our
multiple group membership, and how they shape what we choose to investigate, what sort of data we collect, and what sort of conclusion
we draw from the data that we collect.

Themes and predictions

Having said all of that by way of introduction, I would like to
identify for each of the speakers of this panel what struck me as the
major themes that each speaker was calling to our attention. From
there, I will move to some more general statements about learning in
this area and offer my own set of predictions for the future.

First Jim Reynierse. It seems to me that Jim Reynierse under-
lined and emphasized three major themes. The first had to do with
the expectation of severe competition among overly qualified candi-
dates for a limited number of middle management positions. This certainly suggests that the middle of the organization will be increasingly an arena, which those in charge and those who research will be
stimulated to observe. His second theme is the idea of a major paradox that seems to be emerging in the broader context of organizations. There is a two-fold movement. On the one hand, the economy
seems to be shifting from emphasizing heavy manufacturing to high
technology. There is, and will continue to be, a computer revolution. Along with that technological change, there is also corresponding continuing emphasis on making organizations more humane for the
members. The term we use now is "quality of working life." I am
sure that term will at some point become less fadish and others will
take its place. But the trend toward having organizations be more
responsive to the human properties of members continues even as we
become more of a technological society. Reynierse's third point is

that the human resources planning model is aimed at integrating corporate and individual objectives.

Now, my sense of Jim -- and since I did not check with him in
advance, I could very well be wrong -- but my prediction is that
Reynierse works for a non-unionized organization. His notion of integrating corporate and individual objectives is really not so much
of an integration as it is a cooptation of individuals to transform
themselves in a way that enables them to fully identify with corporate objectives. This raises an interesting question of how behavioral science is used. I imagine that many of you know a number of
companies that have prided themselves in using behavioral science to
keep unions out. Scott Meyers (1971), for example, has written in
the Harvard Business Review that Texas Instruments has used behavioral science in that way, and he advocates it for others. IBM
surely represents another company that has made a fine tradition of
using behavioral science to keep unions out. Given that as a case in
some instances, it is not surprising that there is a great deal of
ambivalence from labor leaders as to whether behavioral science can
really serve the labor movement. They wonder whether it is anything
other than a tactic in labor-management bargaining. I think another
derivative aspect of the Reynierse emphasis on the middle is that not
only does he focus on the problems of middle managers and their
mobility, but he also said we ought to stay out of the top of the
organization. Thus, he does not attempt to take behavioral science
into higher stratospheres of the managerial hierarchy. In his own
words: "It is too political; the Board of Directors handles that."
The net effect, I believe, is to keep behavioral science as very much
of a middle class phenomenon. It does not work with labor and it
does not work with the elite.

Next, I would like to turn to the major themes in what Doug Kuhns
stated. I state the first one in his own words: "There are economic
changes taking place in the current decade that could very well spell
the end of labor relations as we know them." Throughout the Kuhns
paper we notice a theme of major change, or at least the anticipation
of very major change, even to the point of catastrophic magnitudes of
disruption. A related point that he made was in his recalling that
were it not for supplementary unemployment benefits, at least in the
mind of one senior executive, the recession of '74-'75 would have
seen people in the streets. The changing work force and changing
population means that a very significant part of the economy is being
shaped by older people, women, and younger people -- particularly
younger blacks. Another strong assertion that Kuhns made was the
anticipated collapse of Detroit -- which he says could be expected to
occur even if there had been no problem with Japanese automobiles.
The fourth theme that I wish to underline from Kuhns is that new
enterprises in the future will need to have the parties involved in
negotiation deal with the removal of labor resources from one area
and their reinstitution in another. I happen to agree with this

prediction. The implications of it for the conduct of management, on the one hand, and the creation of interesting research problems on the other, are very rich indeed.

Now the last speaker to whom I shall refer is Bernie Bass. His talk was about leadership and management. From his perspective there will be far less toleration of laissez-faire leadership. He makes the statement very carefully. He does not mistake equating less toleration for laissez-faire leadership with subtle endorsement of autocratic behavior. He does make the point that leaders need to be better prepared to set directions and take initiatives. It struck me as particularly significant that he drew from this major point the need for research people to deal simultaneously with leaders and subordinates, and with their rationales and rationalizations for what is happening. Here is evidence of intergroup theory in organizations, at least from the standpoint of organization groups. Bass picks up another trend in which he identifies the change in self-orientation of organization members. The point of departure is that people seem to be increasingly able to recognize their self-interests and are looking for constructive ways to further them in organizations. I agree with that view, but I would point out that that is only part of the change. Bass, for example, says that sensitivity training now focuses on self-awareness and personal growth instead of group dynamics. I think that is a mistake. The new trend in experiential group dynamics -- which is a term I like better than sensitivity training -- is a strong effort to incorporate understanding of race and gender into training.

A third point, deriving from what Bass said, which I think is very important, is the emphasis on task orientation as a dominant theme. I believe the need for effectiveness, productivity, growth in the economy will stay with us for some time, as we attempt to turn the country around, and it will show in the constructions people make as to the purpose of organizational psychology.

My reading of the issues at stake in the future, as it is derived from listening not only to the speakers that have directly preceded me but also from the preceding panel, is that we will be entering a period of remarkable if not catastrophic change. There is hope in this period, but the hope is limited. The polarities that were identified among the speakers include those of the old versus young, male versus female, people changes versus technological changes, economic interpretations versus psychological interpretations, specialist training versus generalist training, black versus white ethnicity, and leadership versus followership. The pessimistic side of the impending radical change is that we will deal with these polarities in traditional ways and that the catastrophy, if it comes, will be fought out in the polarities as just described. The alternative -- and I think that this conference is a good example of the possibility of such an alternative -- is that the traditional polarities become

inverted. That is real change. The issues do not go away, but the
way we think and act about them does become altered substantially.
The more that polarities reverse their usual form, the more opportunity we have for creative thought and useful action. We cannot
escape biases; we can learn to use them fruitfully. Evidence we have
all seen in this room suggests that it is possible. But then there
is also the Reagan-Regan, or Regan-Reagan administration, and its
trend to replace social services with prisons and weapons. This may
bring a tough choice to organizational psychologists. We may have to
decide whether to buy in or die out. If that occurs, it will spell
the end of organizational psychology as we know it today (to borrow a
phrase from Doug Kuhn).

References

Myers, M. S. Overcoming union opposition to job enrichment. <u>Harvard
    Business Review</u>, 1971, <u>49</u>(#), 37-49.
Sheleff, L. S. <u>Generations apart: Adult hostility to youth</u>. New
    York: McGraw-Hill, 1981.

PART IV

HIGHER EDUCATION FOR THE '90's

WE CAN INFLUENCE THE FUTURE!

Dwight W. Allen

Old Dominion University

Norfolk, VA

When we talk about things like the changing composition of the workforce, we are really dealing with future projections. In looking at higher education concerns for the 1990's, one of the problems we have is that the same words mean very different things to different people. We really are not talking the same language, for instance, in terms of our definition of what change is and what composition of the workforce is. We have different definitions of what the workforce is, who is in it, who is out of it, how you prepare to get into it, when you are prepared, and when you are still in preparation. All of these definitions are there to confuse things. In addition, one of the reasons that higher education doesn't change often times is because future predictions are too easily dismissed. Many people don't believe we can study the future. I would argue that we can study the future as easily and as systematically as we can study the past.

It is Right to be Wrong

If you look at the way in which we study the past and the ways in which we make projections and predictions for the future, you will find that the predictions about the past are just about as susceptible to error as predictions about the future. Frances Fitzgerald, a journalist who wrote the Pulitzer prize-winning book, Fire in the Lake, gave herself the task of reading all the elementary and secondary U.S. history books that had been written in the last 100 years. She wanted to see whether a consistent view of U.S. history was presented. She presented some devastating things in her book America Revised. One example is that textbooks have changed three times since 1900 about who won the War of 1812! To cite an example in a different realm, we might think about the Brontosaurus

155

in the British Museum. In 1979, assistant curators in the museum
quietly removed the head of the Brontosaurus and replaced it with
another one. They found that the archeologists had reconstructed
the beast with the wrong head! We used to think, in addition, that
dinosaurs were extinct. The scientific community is now in agreement that they are not extinct -- they are called birds! So, we
have to learn to be more confident about the future, because in the
very same way that people are inclined to be unreasonably certain
about the past, they're inclined to be unreasonably uncertain about
the future.

If I were to ask, "Will the sun rise tomorrow?", you might say,
if you are very intelligent and very sophisticated, "Maybe." If I
asked a simple Indian peasant, "Will the sun rise tomorrow?", the
answer would be "Yes." If you look at the likelihood of the sun
rising tomorrow and make any kind of statistical prediction, it
would look very certain. Yet, because we are dealing with the
future and because we like to give the future a bit of mysticism, we
get into the mindset that it's better to say, "Maybe" than to say
"Yes." If we are willing to say "Maybe" about the sun rising
tomorrow, just think how that might play into other projections we
might make, most particularly about the changing composition of the
workforce.

One of the biggest tasks facing higher education from a practitioner's point of view is to get higher education to use the data
that is available with which to predict the future; to get the professors and administrators of higher education to learn how to give
credibility to the data that we have and to learn what is appropriate credibility. We tend to be inconsistent in terms of how
certain we are about the past, the present and the future. We have
all these water-tight compartments in our minds and we never require
any consistency between the compartments. That is what gets us into
trouble when we try to predict the future of something. We don't
use the data which is available because of these inconsistencies in
the different compartments of our minds.

If, for example, on a scale of one to ten, my certainty about
something that is going to happen in the future is six, then it
isn't a surprise that it doesn't happen. It doesn't discredit the
process. With a correlation of .6, you would be right about 40% of
the time. I suggest that it is better to be right 40% of the time
using data than to be right a random part of the time not using
data. We have to learn how to use data that are at an appropriate
confidence level. I would argue that if we learn how to use that
data, our training programs would be dramatically different than
they are now.

The Dean of the Stanford School of Medicine introduces his new
classes with the statement, "Ladies and gentlemen, half of what you

are about to learn in medical school is already known to be false.
Unfortunately, we don't know which half!" I find that a terribly
important mindset for us to have in higher education. It tells
students that it is appropriate to learn things that might be wrong,
because that is the best we can do. The only thing worse than
learning things that might be wrong is not learning things that
might be wrong. We have a dangerous trend in higher education
where, in the light of changing trends, many programs are being discredited because they might be wrong. Somehow we have to gain back
an appropriate level of credibility for programs that are dealing
with increasing levels of ambiguity.

The latest statistics I saw in the area of computer science, for
example, say that the half-life of the computer scientist is between
two and three years. What that means is simply that within three
years, half of what you learn will be worthless. If the professional half-life of a computer scientist is three years, does that
have implications for a training program? Certainly it does.
Should universities give up training computer scientists, then,
because it takes four years to train a computer scientist whose
half-life is only three years after he gets trained? I maintain
that we have to somehow teach people some sort of humility about
what they know and teach them not to be surprised when what they
know turns out to be modified. This is one of the most important
challenges to higher education I see in the 1990's. We need to
train university teachers to be humble about what they know and what
they don't know, and to communicate this humility to their students.
The alternative is that the training programs we are conducting are
going to come increasingly under attack and become increasingly
discredited.

A trend we are moving toward now is that we are finding more and
more industries who insist on their own training programs and give
minimum lip service to what universities do. I personally think
this trend is partly constructive, because it may drag the universities out of the "ivy halls" into the market place and into society
where they belong. One of my predictions about the changing needs
of higher education in the 1990's is a lot more cottage industry in
higher education and more on-site courses for a variety of purposes.

Problems Higher Education Needs to Confront

Keeping these thoughts in mind, I would isolate six specific
problems that higher education needs to address because of the
changing composition of the workforce.

The Mystique of Occupational Entry Levels. The first is the
problem of entry. There is increasing complexity and specialization
of the work place, and it is much harder for the university to
prepare an increasing range of specialists. In addition, industry

seems to be inconsistent in determining what kind of training it
wants the university to provide, whether specialized or generalist
training which could be supplemented with on-the-job training. One
of the things that has to be analyzed, in my judgment, is the whole
mystique of entry levels. For example, entry level in the law, or
three years of law school, will not allow most people to pass the
bar examination. To pass the bar examination after you have completed a three year law degree, you must take a six week bar review
course. It is well known that you could probably pass the bar examination with only the six week bar review course, if you would be
permitted to take it. It is a guild system, however, which does not
allow people to take that bar review course unless they have completed law school. It can be well documented that engineers, as
another example, use only about 20% of the skills they learn in
undergraduate engineering programs. The fact of the matter is that
higher education personnel do not have a practitioner's viewpoint of
training.

My number one suggestion, then, in terms of how I would like to
see higher education respond in the 1990's, would be to find ways to
bring practitioners systematically into programs of preparation and
to have some sort of rotating association with major practitioners
who would serve an inservice training capacity, particularly in
those fields that change rapidly. These practitioners should be
given senior academic status in order to have an impact. I would
also suggest that a series of clinical or senior professorships be
developed in various fields, perhaps in cooperation on a rotating
basis with major consumers of the products that the university is
training.

What We Do Not Know About Jobs in Year 2000. Another entry
level problem is the fact that we don't know what 50% of the jobs
will be in the year 2000. In other words, 50% of the market place
in the year 2000 is going to contain jobs that have not yet been
dreamed up. Because of the lead time it takes for higher education
to get organized to develop the training programs to put people
through, we would barely be ready if we started right now to train
people for whatever job "x" is going to be in the year 2000. How do
we do that when nobody has told us what job "x" is? This suggests
to me that we're going to have to develop different mechanisms for
the approval, development and administration of training programs.
Perhaps we're going to have to return more substantially to a four
year general education degree with less importance given to a major
and specific training done on-the-job. I would argue that this is
probably as true for engineering as it is for social sciences. I
would argue that if you have a person of high mathematical and
scientific aptitude, I am not at all sure that the kind of program
we put that person through under the guise of professional vocational training is really all that appropriate or important to their
job performance.

Skill Obsolesence. Third, I think higher education is going to
have to deal with the problem of skill obsolescence. This must be
addressed in terms of the way the university reshapes the cottage
industry notion. This suggests that if the universities got organized to have rapid deployment strike forces, they would be able to
go out into the market place to "blitz" industries with appropriate
skill retraining programs. Some of these skill retraining programs
might appropriately be very small modular seminars. We may want to
reconceptualize the whole notion of what degrees are around a different unit of credit which would be more modular than the semester
unit is now.

Universities also need to address the issue of unfulfilling
employment. As the market place tightens, people have less job
mobility in certain kinds of professions, the most notable of which
is teaching, at the elementary, secondary and higher education
levels. People get into a job and feel immobilized. This is one of
the primary sources of unfulfilling employment in the psychological
sense. I would argue that our task in higher education is to help
our society discover the legitimacy of a psychological identity that
is independent of a vocational identity. This could solve many problems at all levels of the society and make a lot of jobs easier to
handle. It would encourage employers to treat their employees dif-
ferently and to be concerned about non-vocational aspects of lifestyle. I cite an example of a friend of mine in Amherst,
Massachusetts. If asked, "What do you do?", his answer would be,
"I'm a poet." If you then asked him, "Where is your poetry published?", his answer would be, "It's not." Depending on whether or
not he liked you, he might add, "...and I earn my living teaching
physics at Amherst College." So here we have a poet who happens to
earn his living teaching physics. A bulldozer operator might make
$30,000-40,000 a year, but we tend to look down our noses at a bull-
dozer operator. If we could unhook the psychological identity of
the bulldozer operator from that vocational identity, we would find
many happier bulldozer operators, because they would not feel they
were being limited by their bulldozing operations. The irony is
that everybody is becoming more unfulfilled in their employment as
the employment market tightens. I would recommend, then, that
higher education and education in general need to address this
problem head on.

Job Obsolescence/Transition. The fourth problem I would like to
identify is the problem of job obsolescence, which I distinguish
from skill obsolescence. Examples might be the buggy whip maker,
firemen on locomotives, or trolley conductors. How do you help
people with job obsolescence? University retraining programs are an
obvious answer, and again I think these retraining programs are
going to do a better job if they are more generalist in nature.
Related to job obsolescence is a fifth area, job transition. I
think universities have a marvelous opportunity to help reduce the

human cost when a person finds him/ herself in an obsolete job. A
timetable ought to be anticipated in order to phase in new skills or
to train people for a completely new profession which is unrelated
to their old profession. One of the things which I find most intri-
guing in terms of career replacement is the person who moves from a
high pressure career where he/she is phased out at an early age, to
a complete reversal where he/she moves to Maine and cuts wood!
There is something psychologically much more satisfying about
choosing a completely different lifestyle which defies comparison
with the old lifestyle. Universities can be enormously helpful in
exploiting some of these psychological circumstances in terms of the
problems of job obsolescence and job transition.

    New Definitions of Retirement. The final challenge, I think, is
the idea of retirement. Here, I think, we have to learn new definitions of "retirement." One of the most serious mistakes that is
made in any kind of career planning or placement is made in the
office of high school counselors. High school counselors tend to
counsel students about preparing for their "career." In fact, evidence shows that the average person will change careers three to
five times in his/her lifetime. High school counselors tend to keep
this a secret. They don't talk to students about training for
careers, or getting out of the first one into the next one. That is
where my new definition of retirement comes in. I believe that some
people should retire from their first career at the age of 22, if
they find themselves in a career that is totally unrewarding. When
we live in a society that is as career mobile as it is, we ought to
be able to do a better job of helping people identify their dissatisfaction and prepare to do something about it. Of course, the more
traditional definitions of retirement come in here also, retirement
from the military being the most obvious example. More and more
people are having second and third careers. Perhaps you know of a
famous philosopher named Whitehead. His career as a philospher took
place after he retired as a scientist. In fact, we don't remember
much about his scientific career at all.

In Summary

    Higher education has some real challenges ahead. We are going
to have to learn how to read the data of the future and how to use
it. This data will include not just demographic data about which
jobs are there, but data that will help people deal psychologically
with the transitions they are likely to face. Higher education
needs a rather thorough overhaul for the 1990's if it is going to
rise to the challenge of those changes which, from my perspective,
has a predictive validity of at least .6.

COLLEGE STUDENT VALUES AND THE WORLD OF WORK

Helen S. Astin

University of California at Los Angeles

Los Angeles, CA

For the past few years, I have been very interested and involved in the questions raised here thus far by my colleagues. That is:

Changes in the population mix of college students today and in the near future

Changes in the value orientations of young people attending college today

Declining enrollments and the implications for higher education

These are some of the parameters that frame my thoughts and my current research efforts.

For our deliberations at this time, I would like to review and highlight some research findings on the following topics:

1. Student values, expectations, and interests.
2. Adult women in higher education.

Very recently I undertook some analysis of college students' values and the relation of these values to their expectations about their future careers. I believe that such an analysis can give us a sense of the type of worker that will enter the labor force in the near future.

Much has been written recently about the changing values of college students. If the students of the 1960s were viewed as radicals who were concerned primarily with political issues, the students of

today have been labeled hedonists and narcissists who care only
about getting good-paying jobs that will enable them to live
comfortably.   Social conscience, it is said, has given way to a new
vocationalism.

Yankelovich, in a recent article, labeled young people of today
"a New Breed of Americans," whose values and beliefs differ so much
from the traditional that

....they promise to transform the character of work in
America....   Three of the more striking manifestations of
New Breed work-related values are (1) the increasing importance of leisure, (2) the symbolic significance of the paid
job, and (3) the insistence that jobs become less deperson-
alized (Yankelovich, 1978, p. 47).

With respect to the first, he points out that of the three concerns
that usually dominate people's lives and compete for their time and
attention -- family life, work, and leisure -- the first two have
gradually assumed less importance, and the third more.   Among women,
however, and mostly as a result of the women's movement that began
in the 1960s, holding a paid job has become increasingly important
as a symbol of independence and autonomy.   But the young people of
today do not expect to define themselves primarily through the kind
of work they do.   They look upon jobs as a means of self-
fulfillment, and they emphasize working with pleasant people.
Yankelovich concludes that the incentives in the world of work must
be revamped to fit these altered work motivations.

In an annual meeting of the American Association for Higher
Education, Rosabeth Moss Kanter described the dramatic changes taking place among college students:

If the cultural ethos of the 1960's could be phrased in
terms of quality, that of today's students would be described by some analysts in terms of quantity: a concern
for accumulation; for entry into high-paying occupations;
for knowing how many jobs exist in the first place and for
making oneself marketable with respect to them....   In
fact, both quality and quantity are expected....   We hear
simultaneously the desire for enough, for more, and for
better (Kanter, 1978, p. 1).

In short, according to Kanter, the workers of tomorrow will both demand and expect more of their jobs.

Student Values, Expectations, and Interests

These are some examples of how commentators view today's young
people.   What I have tried to do was to test the validity of their

perceptions against data that have been collected from college
students since 1966. From these data comes information on trends in
students' career plans, as well as in their goals, values and attitudes. I will deal with three questions in particular. First, why
do students attend college? More specifically, do students today
look at a college education as a way to increase their general knowledge and to develop an appreciation of ideas or simply as a way to
prepare for the world of work? Second, are students becoming less
socially concerned and more personally and selfishly oriented? That
is, as they look into the future, are they more likely to set a high
priority on such goals as contributing to society and helping
others, or such goals as fulfilling themselves and enhancing their
own resources? Third -- and most directly related to the theme of
this conference -- what implications do their values have for the
world of work in the future?

Before I try to answer these questions, let me remind you that,
even today, half of the students now in college are the first generation in their families to go beyond high school. Let me remind
you too that the traditional college-age population (the 18 to 21
year olds) is shrinking. Moreover the sex and racial/ethnic composition of the college cohort is changing. The proportion of women
among entering college freshmen has increased steadily in recent
years, as has the proportion of minority students. And these increases are likely to continue for a variety of reasons. For
example, California anticipates a 40 percent decline in the number
of white high school graduates by the mid-1980's. The graduating
classes of the Los Angeles public high schools are expected to be
about 40 percent white and 60 percent nonwhite by 1985. And these
demographic changes are bound to have an impact on the kinds of
college-educated workers in tommorrow's labor market. Thus, it is
worthwhile to examine some of the similarities and differences
between the sexes and among racial/ethnic groups with respect to
career plans and expectations, since such an analysis may throw more
light on what we can expect of the college-educated workers of
tomorrow.

First, I would like to review for you some trends over time with
respect to values, attitudes, and interests. The data on these
trends are drawn from the responses of entering freshmen to a survey
questionnaire administered through the Cooperative Institutional
Research Program (CIRP) of the American Council of Education and
University of California at Los Angeles, which began in 1966. The
CIRP involves a representative sample of the nation's colleges and
universities "The American Freshman: Natural Norms". That sample
now numbers approximately 600. The entire first-time, full-time
cohort of freshmen at each participating institution is surveyed
annually, and the data thus collected are weighted to represent the
universe of entering college freshmen.

Reasons for Going to College. In recent CIRP surveys, entering
freshmen were asked to indicate their reasons for going to college.
Twelve possible reasons were listed, including "my parents wanted me
to go," "to be able to get a better job," "to make me a more cul-
tured person," and "there was nothing better to do." Our comparison
years are 1976 and 1978. Even though the time-span is not long
enough, differences between the two years in the proportions indicating that a given reason was very important to them deserve some
mention, as do differences between the sexes.

First, to give the general picture: The top-ranked reasons are
generally the same for both years and (with one exception) for both
sexes. More than half the entering freshmen said they went to college to learn more about things that interested them, to be able to
get a better job, and to gain a general education and appreciation
of ideas. In both years, men were more likely to say that they were
attending college in order to be able to make more money, whereas
women were more likely to cite the opportunity to meet new and interesting people.

The reasons least likely to be cited as very important (checked
by fewer than one-tenth of both sexes in both years) were having
nothing better to do, not being able to find a job, and wanting to
get away from home. In short, students attend college because they
want to be there, not because of negative incentives.

There was an increase in the proportion who said they were attending college for the very practical purposes of getting a better
job and making more money and that increase was greater among women
than among men. This finding would seem to confirm Yankelovich's
assertion that getting a paid job is taking on greater symbolic significance among women, as well as the contention of many observers
that women are coming to assume more male-typed goals and values.

Nonetheless, this analysis does not support the notion that students in the 1970's went to college just to insure that they would
get better jobs and make more money: Young people were also likely
to cite intrinsic motivations: learning about things that interest
them and gaining general knowledge and an appreciation of ideas.

Career Choices. What are the career choices of entering freshmen, and how have they changed over time? The most dramatic increase -- for both sexes, but especially for women -- has occurred
in the choice of business as a career. In 1966, 19 percent of the
male entering freshmen cited this career choice; by 1979 the figure
had risen to 23 percent. Only 3 percent of the 1966 female freshmen
named this career choice; over the years, the proportion increased
steadily, rising to 17 percent in 1979.

The most dramatic decreases were registered for the career
choices of elementary and secondary school teacher. Also declining

in popularity over the years as freshman career choices were the
occupations of college professor and of research scientist.

Another notable finding to emerge in this trend analysis is the
increase in the number of women who as freshmen planned on careers
in fields formerly regarded as male domain such as physician, lawyer
and engineer.

The career choices in allied health professions peaked in popularity for both men and women in the mid-1970's, then declined
slightly. Another observation I would like to relate is that occupational segregation of the sexes seems to occur over time. Men
initially choosing female-typed occupations defect from those
choices, as do women initially choosing male-typed careers. The
main exceptions among women are the career choices of business and
law. Thus, despite the undoubted impact of the women's movement,
the break from the traditional may not be so sharp as some commentators have suggested, at least insofar as career choice is concerned.

Life Goals. The long-term goals that people set for themselves
reflect their basic values. What are the life goals of college students; have they changed over time; and if so, in what ways?
Answers to these questions can provide valuable insights into the
values of tomorrow's workers. Trend data on those life goals that
entering freshmen consider essential or very important are available
from the CIRP freshman surveys throughout the 1970's.

Of the list of 17 life goals, those ranking at the top and those
ranking at the bottom are generally the same across time for both
sexes. Thus, over half the entering freshmen in all years considered, from 1972 to 1979, have set a high priority on becoming an
authority in their fields, raising a family, and helping others in
difficulty. In addition, over half the men (but not the women) say
that succeeding in a business of their own is very important to
them. The lowest-ranking goals across the years (cited by fewer
than one in five) are connected with artistic accomplishments --
achieving in a performing art, writing original works, and creating
artistic works such as painting and sculpture -- and with
influencing the political structure.

The most notable decline over time has occurred with respect to
the goal of developing a meaningful philosophy of life. One goal
that has increased in importance for both sexes is that of obtaining
recognition from colleagues for contributions to one's special
field. Other goals that have increased in popularity among both
sexes are having administrative responsibility, making a theoretical
contribution to science, becoming an authority in a field, and being
very well-off financially; the increase in the proportion endorsing
these last two goals was particularly marked among women. In addition, women -- but not men -- have become much more likely to say

that succeeding in their own business is very important to them. All these goals cluster together in a dimension I have labeled materialistic/status, and reflect a growing emphasis on such rewards.

Becoming involved in projects to clean up the environment has become a less important goal for both sexes. What are some of the conclusions we may draw from these trend data? It is not necessarily true that students are becoming less altruistic (the proportions endorsing the goal of helping others in difficulty registered an overall drop of only four percentage points between 1972 and 1979 for both sexes) or placing less value on family life (the proportions subscribing to the goal of raising a family rose slightly for both sexes; men were only slightly less likely than women to rate this goal as very important). Nonetheless, an increasing interest in material success (being financially well-off) and in status goals (winning recognition, becoming an authority in a field, having administrative responsibility) is evident, especially among women, who would seem to be adopting the values of men. Equally obvious is a declining interest in political issues and social action.

Sex and Racial/Ethnic Differences in Values. Next, I would like to discuss differences between men and women among racial/ethnic groups in three areas of concern: (1) education values (as reflected in reasons for going to college), (2) work values (as reflected in reasons for career choice), and (3) life goals.

In going to college, women, independent of their racial or ethnic background, are more likely to be motivated by reasons related to educational and social development. Men, on the other hand, cite reasons related to job preparation and passive acceptance. However, more whites than blacks went to college for reasons related to fulfillment of expectations, and more blacks than whites mentioned side benefits such as participating in special programs or getting financial aid. Job preparation was much more often a consideration for black than for white women, whereas white women -- as well as white men -- indicated that college attendance represented fulfillment of expectations.

In choosing a career, women are more likely than men to have a job (as opposed to a career) orientation; to be intrinsically motivated and to have a service orientation. Conversely, men more often cite reasons related to need for autonomy. Whites are less likely than are blacks and Chicanos to have a service orientation.

In summary, the findings about sex differences reported here are not particularly surprising in view of past research showing that women tend to value the intrinsic aspects of work, and to have a service orientation. Further, it is not surprising that women have a job rather than a career orientation. Only recently have women begun to think in terms of long-term careers; traditionally, women worked right after college, before their children were born, and after their children had grown up, and the wife's work was subordinate to that of her husband. Even though the women's movement has changed this thinking to some extent, many women still espouse the traditional view. Supporting this conclusion is the finding that women tend to look at education as an end in itself rather than as a means to an end; that is, a way of preparing for a career. Despite these sex differences, however, men and women were very similar in their tendency to go to college for reasons related to fulfillment of expectations, and in the value they placed on the extrinsic rewards of an occupation. Thus, women are much more likely to have both extrinsic and intrinsic work values, whereas men tended to be motivated almost exclusively by extrinsic considerations.

With regard to work values, blacks and Chicanos, compared to whites, are more likely to be motivated by extrinsic/pragmatic considerations and to have a service orientation. In addition, blacks place higher value on materialistic/status goals than do either whites or Chicanos.

These findings suggest the following:

1) Women are becoming more like men in the values they espouse and in their career plans.

2) More minorities entering higher education bring with them different values.

However, the question still remains whether they are going to shift their value orientation and become more like the dominant group. A need to monitor these trends in value orientation should continue to be important since students with different value orientations appear to aspire to different careers.

Values and Career Plans. In addition to trends, we also examined the relationship of these values to career plans. In a sense we asked: how do different work values translate into specific career choices? We find that students manifesting a pragmatic/extrinsic orientation are most likely to plan on careers in accounting, business, law and engineering but unlikely to plan on careers in teaching. Those manifesting a strong need for autonomy tend to choose careers in business or law but not teaching or medicine. Those with a strong service orientation typically plan on careers in medicine but not in accounting or engineering.

Before I leave this topic, let me share a couple of observations about the values, attitudes and expectations of college men and women today. A couple of years ago we did a study on the nature of the educational experience of men and women attending coeducational and single sex institutions (Astin & Kent, 1980).

In that study, we observed that an important difference between women and men and one that could prove to be a source of conflict involved sex-role ideology, especially attitudes toward the employment of women. Two-thirds of the women wanted full time careers, whereas only two-fifths of the men indicated that they wanted their partners to work full time.

Moreover, men were more likely to believe that mothers of preschool children should not work outside the home. Thus, whereas sex-roles are changing, men are still lagging behind -- moreover, the sexes are not talking about these issues. Newspaper columnist Ellen Goodman labeled this communication gap a <u>conspiracy of silence</u>. She wisely observes that on campuses across the country women's issues are largely a single-sex subject.

Adult Women and Higher Education

Even though institutions of higher education have opened their doors to a new population of nontraditional students; older persons, housewives, second-careerists, very little research has been done on the specific needs and interests of these populations or about their personal characteristics and modes of learning.

In the early 1970's we undertook a national study of adult women in higher education. The study was designed to examine the needs, interests, aspirations, goals and views of adult women about education and work. The study also addressed the complex interactions between familial variables and educational and occupational outcomes. The results of that study have been published in a book entitled <u>Some Action of Her Own</u> (Astin, 1976). However, let me briefly share with you some of these findings.

Continuing education programs for women were originally developed to facilitate the entry or re-entry of women past the traditional age of 18, into the academic world. Some of the barriers for re-entry women were both personal and institutional: The first problem is how to go about returning to school or beginning a career. Another problem is the lack of confidence a person experiences after being out of school for some time. Arranging a schedule to include both academic and home responsibilities is another problem. These barriers continue to exist and Continuing Education Programs for Women have managed to deal with them and to try to reduce them.

Higher education can take lessons from these programs in dealing effectively with the needs and interests of adults entering or reentering higher education. There is a need for:

1. Finding ways to assess past records, some ten to twenty years old;

2. The development of flexible curricula as to time and place;

3. Transferability of credit; and

4. Financial aid.

Research

Some of the discussion that has already taken place at this conference about issues of work and family, sexual harassment, role
overload, burn out, affluent drop out, and communication gap lead me
to believe that an important area of research should be on the
nature of friendship, relationships and colleagueships in the work
place.

Moreover, women's changing aspirations and pursuit of nontraditional careers suggest the need for research on the integration of
women in the work place, on the importance of ratio of women to men
and its effects on productivity and job satisfaction; the importance
of networking and mentoring for women in nontraditional work settings also needs to be examined. Also, the changing values and aspirations of women raise the following questions for me: Do women
have to adapt to male values to be able to enter and succeed in the
traditionally male occupations? Do their values change first, or do
they choose to enter these new, for them, fields first and then make
shifts in their values in order to survive?

Three areas meriting additional research to enlarge our understanding of issues in career choice and development of women
include:

1. Monitoring the trends in choices, preferences, aspirations
and the actual behavior of women must continue now and in the generations to come. This time period is critical to women's social
and economic roles. Changes in the behavior, expectations, and preferences of women have already occurred. College women's attitudes
are shifting toward a preference for and expectation of performing
career and homemaking roles simultaneously. Changes in institutional arrangements, family, education, and work should permit women to
combine these roles more easily and to continue in their careers
with only minor interruptions.

2. Variables that characterize women with certain career
choices and variables that enhance or inhibit career development
must be better identified. The personal characteristics of women
and the early experiences that affect the choice and pursuit of
different fields and careers must be determined. Studies can
utilize crossectional populations; the plans, choices, preparation
and entry of women of different ages, ethnic backgrounds and socioeconomic status should be more thoroughly explored. We need to know

more about the differentiating characteristics, early developmental
experiences, and educational experiences of women in different
fields and with different employers. For example, who are the women
in the sciences, what were their early experiences? What has made
possible their better preparation in math and science?

3. More intensive longitudinal efforts must be made to identify
the critical experiences in the lives of young women which result in
differential abilities and personality traits, all important deter-
minants in career choice and development. For example, how do young
children begin to formulate concepts about work and about themselves? What kinds of home environments and parent-child interactions develop autonomy, high self-esteem and a sense of competence
in a variety of areas? What educational experiences reinforce a
sense of self-worth and competence? What role does a liberal arts
program, a work-and-study experience, career guidance, or specialized math curricula play in the development of interests, motivations and competencies essential to appropriate career choice and
development?

These studies should be couched in the context of social institutions. In examining the developmental aspects of women and work,
the various institutional practices that affect women's full development and utilization must also be examined in greater depth.

Last let me briefly suggest another important area of research
that takes into consideration age and gender as they relate to productivity. It has to do with faculty research productivity and how
age and gender affect it. Earlier in our deliberations, Sheppard
mentioned the "folklore" that increased age leads to lower productivity. There is also a concern about the health of the research
enterprise as a result of the tenured-in faculty and the decline in
job opportunities in the academic labor market. There is some research that indicates that productivity is high in the beginning of
one's career and before retirement, with a decline and a plateau in
the middle years. We need to examine the relationship of age to
productivity separately for each field. What are the reasons for
women's lower research productivity and more importantly, why do
women receive less colleague recognition and have less visibility
even when they are as productive as are the men? These questions of
age and gender in relationship to faculty productivity remain critical and in need of further exploration.

References

Astin, H. S. (Ed.). Some action of her own: the adult woman and
    higher education. Lexington, Mass: D. C. Heath, 1976.

Astin, H. S., & Kent, L. The development of relatedness and
    autonomy in the college years, in Men and women learning
    together: a study of college students in the late 1970's.
    Providence, R.I.: Brown University, 1980.
Kanter, R. M. Changing shape of work: psychosocial trends in
    America. Current Issues in Higher Education, 1978, 1-8.
Yankelovich, D. The new psychological contracts of work.
    Psychology Today, May 1978, 47-50.

WHOM SHOULD THE SCHOOLS SERVE, WHEN...?

John W. Moore

Old Dominion University

Norfolk, VA

My professional experience has been mainly in old established colleges and universities. Those more traditional institutions were content with what they had become, and were not very interested in changing. So, when the opportunity to join Old Dominion came my way, I jumped at it. I thought it would be a valuable experience to be a part of a relatively new developing institution. All of my expectations have been realized.

At ODU I assumed a role that had a planning dimension. It proved to be an interesting challenge and I struggled with that role for the first year or so. One day, in the mail, I received a two or three page memorandum from a recently appointed Eminent Professor of Psychology by the name of Glickman, in which he listed a whole series of ideas and trends that he thought a university like Old Dominion ought to be taking into account in its planning, and at the very end of that memorandum he raised the question, "Is Old Dominion ready for the challenges of 1990?" When I first started reading the memo, I was delighted to get it because I really hadn't found very many faculty members who were particularly interested in planning the future of the university. Now, finally, I found one who was interested and yet that last question, "Are we ready, are we prepared to deal with the challenges of the 1990's?" frightened me because I had to honestly answer that I wasn't sure that we were.

Six months later I received another memorandum very much like the first one, only longer, from another eminent professor, Dwight Allen. Professor Allen's memorandum basically suggested some of the same questions as Professor Glickman's. This time I was quite anxious about the answer because I was convinced that "no, the University is not ready for the 1990's," and we needed to get busy preparing for the future.

173

At the outset of the talk, I have to confess to you that I have guarded optimism about the value of systematic and rational long range planning in complex universities. I will acknowledge that the introduction of new approaches to planning and management in higher education during the past ten years has been a positive development. Today, administrators are much more conscious of the nature of and the need for effective planning and management. But I do think there has also been a tendency to over sell "planning" and to be unrealistic about results of such long range processes.

If planning means predicting the future, I'm very skeptical about its value. If planning means developing strategic long range master planning documents, I am also very skeptical of that. If, on the other hand, planning means making today's decisions with a full understanding of the implications of those decisions for the future of the University, then I think planning can be very helpful. My orientation in planning is to place emphasis on today's decisions as they relate to the future. Therefore, I don't think you can make today's decisions well unless you think about significant societal trends and environmental forces such as those suggested by Professors Astin and Allen.

Now, I would like to suggest to you some of the trends or environmental forces which I think higher education has to pay some attention to. And I'm going to do this rather rapidly because I think to some extent I'm going to be repeating things that others have said before me.

First, I think that one of the trends that is occurring in our environment about which there is little argument, is the rapid social and technological change is part of our daily lives and it relates to the concepts of job and skill obsolescence that Professor Allen referred to. This rapid change will contribute to increasing demand for training and post-secondary education.

Another significant trend that we are accommodating in our planning today relates to the changing nature of the population that colleges and universities will be serving. During the past two days, we have referred to important demographic shifts in the population. The society is growing older, and colleges and universities will be serving fewer students from the traditional 18-20 age cohort. We will be serving an older, more experienced student population. The so called "non-traditional student".

Higher education will also be effected by the changing role of women, minorities and other ethnic groups in our society. Our obligations to serve these groups will be increasing.

We have also discussed the significant changes in the workforce that will place even greater emphasis on continuous re-training and

education of personnel. Education and training are becoming life
long processes. Changes in the labor market will effect higher
education.

As higher education plans for the future, we will recognize
that, although the population is becoming older and more diverse,
the demand for training and education is likely to continue to increase at very significant rates. I think there will be opportunities for higher education in the future, which many of my colleagues
in higher education are failing to recognize. Some of us are too
preoccupied with the projected decline in enrollment in the 18-22
year old age bracket, without recognizing that beyond that group is
a very substantial service population that will have continuing
needs for training and education and other forms of human
development.

These demographic shifts offer great opportunity and challenge
for higher education in the 80's and 90's. We have to direct our
attention more positively to these trends and focus less on the
negative implications of having fewer younger people coming to our
universities.

Another important development in our society, which I think
colleges and universities are failing to take into account, is that
there is going to be very, very keen competition for students.
Competition that goes beyond the competition among colleges and
universities, but competition for students that will exist among
colleges and universities, proprietary schools, government, and the
private sector. We have statistics today which already tell us that
there are more people engaged in post secondary education in government and the private sector than in our colleges and universities.
Higher education must be aware of this development. If we fail to
meet the needs of our changing society, there are agencies of
government, and in the private sector, that are prepared to do the
job themselves.

It is also clear that during the next decade we will be faced
with the problem of increasing costs of operation. For some reason,
faculty and students on college campuses and members of the society
at large have the opinion that universities are exempt from the
effects of double digit inflation. At a very difficult meeting of
our Board of Visitors last week, we proposed a 16% hike in tuition
and had hundreds of students turn out to debate that issue.
Similarly, university faculty have a great deal of difficulty understanding what is happening to our budgets and our inability to provide the resources that faculty need to do their work well.
Clearly, the costs of higher education are increasing, and it
appears that our public policy is shifting in the direction that
government is interested in laying the costs of higher education on
the students rather than the general public.

I think this represents a very significant change in public policy, and is best reflected in changes being proposed by the Reagan administration that are affecting our student assistance programs. These changes, if enacted, will have very dramatic effects on the composition of the student bodies of our colleges and universities.

There is another trend at work which disturbs me greatly, and one which I ask your help in reversing. I am referring to the diminishing sense of confidence and interest in education at all levels that is developing in our country today. How many political leaders do you really hear talking about education as a high priority in their political platforms? I don't hear very many. I think this is terribly unfortunate in light of the changes in the work force which suggest that education and training has to continue to be a central priority in our nation, in order for us to be able to cope with the many challenges that lie ahead.

In the public sector, we are, unfortunately, affected by increasing governmental red tape and regulation which makes things like planning and response to changing conditions extremely difficult to do well. We have the problem not only at the national level but also at the state level.

In summary, I think the trends to which I have referred, particularly the uncertainty of public and financial support, are contributing to substantial uncertainty and insecurity in American higher education today. This suggests that colleges and universities planning activities and decision-making processes will have to place a very high emphasis on flexibility and adaptability in response to the needs of its changing non-traditional clientele.

Let me now raise several issues which I think higher education will have to deal with during the immediate future.

Perhaps the most fundamental policy question which we in higher education must address, is the question of whom should we serve in the coming decade? We still are debating the desirability of serving student other than the 18 to 22 age group! Some institutions of higher education are still committed to serving only this conventional population. The other alternative, of course, is to look to the non-traditional student population as perhaps the primary service population of the future. I think that it is essential that we come to terms with what we believe to be our obligations to this older and more diverse student population.

Critical policy issues related to access and matriculation need to be resolved. I think we need to move away from the principle of exclusion to a principle of inclusion, as we develop our admission and matriculation policies. Far too often we have chosen a

principle of exclusion as the measure of the quality of institutions
of higher education. We have placed insufficient value on including
those who need to be served. Patterns of student matriculation must
be allowed to be much more diverse and varied. We need to be prepared to serve the part-time student and the student who can only
attend the university in the evening or on weekends. We need to be
prepared to serve the student who cannot matriculate on a continuous
basis. Some students will need to "stop in" and "stop out" with
some regularity.

We are not prepared today in most institutions to operate with
flexibility in order to make it possible for non-traditional students to attend the university and to reap the benefits of that
opportunity. Institutions need to change the manner in which they
deliver services to students. I'm afraid that many of us have grown
very comfortable teaching our courses in the same mode year in and
year out. We're not very interested in being available for evening
instruction and not excited about being involved in off-campus instruction. Unfortunately, there are not sufficient incentives to
take instructional programs to the student in their place of employment, which I think is something we need to do. We're not very
skillful in the use of telecommunications as a vehicle to deliver
educational services at off-site locations.

All of these ideas, which many of you have heard before, relate
to the manner of delivery, and I think have potential value if
colleges and universities are courageous enough to give them a try.
If we are, in fact, serving as diverse a student population as the
data seem to suggest, I think we need to be prepared to recognize
that we need multiple options for students. I was reading last
night, in the Chronicle of Higher Education, about the new core
curriculum at Harvard. The emerging discussions of the return to
the core curriculum bothers me greatly because I think it's taking
us back in the direction of believing that there is one form of education suitable for all students. I think that is a narrow idea
because it fails to recognize the diversity of the population that
we are serving. Instead, we need to be prepared to figure out ways
of designing curriculum experiences on an individualized basis for
students as much as we possibly can. We also need to correct the
old trap of believing that students can be educated in four years.
Patricia Cross' idea of "life long education" is more appropriate to
the changing world we live in. I would go so far, I think, as
agreeing that there are certain tools of learning, communication
skills, skills in quantitative analysis and that sort of thing,
which are, in fact, basic to all learners. But I doubt that I would
go very much further.

It is also going to be important that our colleges and universities be prepared to place a much higher priority on life and career
planning services for students. This is an area that some

institutions have taken seriously, and are doing an excellent job of working not only with young students, but with adult students who are trying to make critical choices about the way they want to live their lives, and how their educational experience will fit into that plan. I hope that many of us will look to life and career planning as a very, very significant service which we need to provide.

Colleges and universities also need to examine their concept and standards of quality. We need a whole new set of values and definitions regarding how we evaluate what we do and the judgments we make about it. We've been reluctant, I think, to do in the direction of evaluating what we do on the basis of performance. We've been hung up on input measures rather than looking at what's really going on in our programs.

In the future, there will be an opportunity for the development of educational networks among institutions of higher education, the private sector, and government for the purpose of offering joint educational and training programs. There is a great potential for a very profitable marriage between specialists in higher education and their colleagues in the private and public sectors.

One of the most challenging problems that will confront higher education during the difficult times that are ahead is that of how to effectively retain, utilize, motivate, and reward faculty work force. Most colleges and universities do not systematically examine faculty personnel policies and practices, nor do they have well organized faculty development programs. The steady state conditions that will characterize higher education in the future, will require that administrators pay much more attention to creative ways of effectively utilizing their most important resource -- the faculty. Let me conclude then, by saying that the great present danger to American higher education is that people in academic leadership positions seem to be developing very pessimistic attitudes about the 1980's. There is a preoccupation with immediate crises that doesn't allow much time to think beyond the next year or two. The 1990's are not being discussed in any serious way.

I think it's terribly important that those of us in higher education recognize that, although we are facing tough times, we still have great opportunities to make very significant contributions to the society if we're willing to make changes in the way we do business, if we're willing to serve the people who need to be served in ways that meet their needs rather than our own vested interests. Leaders in higher education must find ways of looking beyond the press of today's business in order to more effectively plan for tomorrow's challenges. I believe we are capable of doing what needs to be done -- it is simply a matter of commitment, persistence, and effort.

PARTICIPANTS

Dr. C. J. Adkins, Jr.
Psychology Department
Old Dominion University
Norfolk, VA 23508

Dr. Dwight W. Allen
University Professor of Arts
   and Letters
Old Dominion University
Norfolk, VA 23508

Dr. Clayton P. Alderfer
School of Organization and
   Management
Yale University
56 Hillhouse Avenue
New Haven, CN 06520

Dr. Paul Andrisani
Associate Professor of
   Industrial Relations
School of Business Admin.
Temple University
Philadelphia, PN 19122

Dr. Helen S. Astin
Graduate School of Education
UCLA
Hilgard Avenue
Los Angeles, CA 90024

Mr. William J. Banis
Director, Career Planning
   and Placement
Old Dominion University
Norfolk, VA 23508

Dr. Bernard Bass
School Of Management/SUNY BGM
Binghamton, NY 13901

Dr. Steven R. Berman
Training Director
SFD-NCPD/Dept of Navy
Bldg A-67 Naval Station
Norfolk, VA 23511

Dr. Barbara W. Berry
Director, Personnel and
   Human Resources
Farm Fresh
3487 Inventors Road
Norfolk, VA 23502

Dr. Samuel Bieber
Vice President,
   Academic Affairs
Old Dominion University
Norfolk, VA 23508

Dr. James A. Calliotte
Director, Counseling Center
Old Dominion University
Norfolk, VA 23508

Dr. Thomas G. Carroll
Team Leader, Youth Learning
   and Work
National Institute of Education
1200 19th Street, N.W.
Washington, D.C. 20208

LCOL Alfred M. Coke
Associate Professor
Armed Forces Staff College
7800 Hampton Blvd
Norfolk, VA 23511

Jamshid Dabayhmanesh
4778 Mandan Road
Virginia Beach, VA 23452

Dr. Thomas N. Daymont
Senior Research Associate
Center for Human Resource
   Research
Ohio State University
Columbus, OH 43085

Dr. Glenn L. DeBiasi
Director, Management and
   Organizational Development
Medical Center Hospitals
600 Gresham Drive
Norfolk, VA 23507

Mrs. Fran C. Dennis
Associate Director of
   Personnel
Old Dominion University
Norfolk, VA 23508

Ms. Marian J. Edwards
Manager, Management Development
   Human Relations
Boeing Computer Services Co.
177 Madison Avenue
Morristown, NJ 07960

Dr. Sidney A. Fine
4330 East/West Highway
Bethesda, MD 20014

Dr. Kevin Geoffroy
Professor, School of Education
William and Mary
Williamsburg, VA 23185

Dr. Albert S. Glickman
Psychology Department
Old Dominion University
Norfolk, VA 23508

Marilyn Gordon-Ross
St. Luke's Hospital
1320 Wisconsin Avenue
Racine, WI 53403

Dr. R. D. Hedberg
Asst Vice President –
   Personnel Administration
Southern Railway
Box 1808
Washington, D.C. 20013

Dr. Louis H. Henry
Economics Dept
Old Dominion University
Norfolk, VA 23508

Ms. Mary F. Jackson
Citibank
2200 Grand Avenue #2F
Bronx, NY 10453

Judy Johnson
659 Minute Men Road
Virginia Beach, VA 23462

Dr. Michael J. Kavanagh
Psychology Department
Old Dominion University
Norfolk, VA 23508

Ms. Mary L. Lozano
Office of Personnel Mgmt
1900 E. Street, N.W.
Washington, D.C. 20415

Dr. Wilson W. Kimbrough, Jr.
University of Arkansas
Psychology Dept
3110 Mt. Comfort Road
Fayetteville, AK 72701

Diane Marine
4705 Gosnold Avenue
Norfolk, VA 23508

Dr. Raymond H. Kirby
Chairman, Psychology Dept
Old Dominion University
Norfolk, VA 23508

Dr. R. Bruce McAfee
917 Stockbridge Drive
Virginia Beach, VA 23464

Dr. Abraham K. Korman
Baruch College, CUNY
Dept of Psychology
17 Lexington Avenue
New York, NY 10010

Mr. Kevin McElroy
Advanced Technology Inc.
Penbroke IV, Suite 225
Virginia Beach, VA 23462

Dr. E. D. Kuhns
International Assoc. of
  Machinists & Aerospace
  Workers
1300 Connecticut Avenue, N.W.
Washington, D.C. 20036

Dr. Allen E. McMichael
McMichael & Associates
P.O. Box 64880
Virginia Beach, VA 23464

Mr. Wright Leathers
Principal Analyst,
Advanced Technology, Inc.
1827 Duke of York Quay
Virginia Beach, VA 23454

LCOL Michael D. Mierau
Director for Leadership
  Studies and Training
Armed Forced Staff College
7800 Hampton Blvd
Norfolk, VA 23511

Dr. Richard Leone
Temple University
School of Business Admin
1945 N. Broad St., 2nd Fl.
Philadelphia, PN 19122

Dr. David Moers
Chief, Office of Personnel
  Management
Room 3305
1900 E Street N.W.
Washington, D.C. 20415

Ms. Kay Monte-White
Acting Supervisor, Productivity
  Research Division/Social
  Scientist
Office of Personnel Management
1900 E Street N.W.
Washington, D.C. 20013

Mr. David Robertson
Navy Personnel R & D Center
Code 310
San Diego, CA 92154

Dr. John Moore
Vice President, Educational
  Services & Planning
Old Dominion University
Norfolk, VA 23508

Dr. Bill Schiemann
Vice President, Employee
  Relations Programs
Opinion Research Corp.
N. Harrison Street
Princeton, NJ 08540

Dr. Veronica F. Nieva
The Urban Institute
2100 M Street N.W.
Washington, D.C. 20037

Dr. Harold L. Sheppard
National Council On Aging
1828 L Street N.W.
Washington, D.C. 20036

Dr. James P. O'Brien
Professor of Psychology
Tidewater Community College
520 Talbot Hall Road
Norfolk, VA 23505

Dr. H. Wallace Sinaiko
Program Director, Manpower
  Research & Advisory Services
Smithsonian Institute
801 N. Pitt Street
Alexandria, VA 22314

Ms. Katherine Callaway Patterson
Women's Center
1505 W. 49th Street
Old Dominion University
Norfolk, VA 23508

Dr. Kevin M. Sweeney
American Center for Quality
  of Work Life
3301 New Mexico Avenue, N.W.
Suite 202
Washington, D.C. 20016

Dr. James H. Reynierse
Human Resources Planning Officer
Virginia National Bank
3rd Floor, 1 Commercial Place
Norfolk, VA 23501

Dr. R. W. Swezey
Director, Behavioral Sciences
  Research Center
Science Applications Inc.
1710 Goodridge Drive
McLean, VA 22101

Dr. Mary L. Tenopyr
Manager, Research, Human
  Resources Utilization,
  AT&T, Rm 4B 48
1776 On the Green
Morristown, NJ 07960

Dr. Alma G. Vasquez
Route 29 North--Fed. Executive Inst.
Charlottesville, VA 22903

Mr. Louis P. Willemin
Retired Personnel Research
  Psychology, ARI
11028 Burnley Terrace
Silver Spring, MD 20902

INDEX

Abilities
  managers and supervisors,
      114, 136
  mature workers, 37-39
  older workers, 50-54, 64
  women, 5, 71, 75, 94, 96-97,
      170
  youth, 34, 128
Accidents and safety, 5, 40,
      51, 62
Attitudes, beliefs,
      motivations,
      perceptions and values
  analysis by
    age, 15-18, 28-32, 51, 55,
      61, 146, 162
    college students, 161-170
    family status, 27-32
    income level, 27-32
    race, 28-31, 166-167
    sex, 28-32, 76, 91, 99,
      161-170
  concerning
    achievement, 108-109
    affiliation, 107-109
    aged and aging, 15-18,
      50-52, 54, 56, 61, 64,
      146
    alienation, 107
    ambition, 33, 60
    aspirations, 40, 83, 162,
      169
    autonomy, 59, 162
    career choice, 94, 162,
      164-167, 169
    college attendance, 163-166

Attitudes, beliefs,
      motivations,
      perceptions and values
      (continued)
  concerning (continued)
    equal opportunity, 99
    expectations, 10-12, 138,
      162-163
    family and home, 11, 32,
      83-89, 107, 162
    financial security, 89
    hierarchy of values, 99
    incentives, 25-32, 42
    initiative, 28, 30
    interaction, 137
    job satisfaction, 5, 11,
      27-29, 40, 49, 54-56,
      59, 60, 63, 73-76, 83,
      85, 114, 159, 169
    leisure, 11, 57-58, 114,
      162
    life goals, 162, 165-166
    occupational prestige,
      94-95, 159
    personal development, 11,
      137
    race, 15, 145-146, 150
    retirement, 16-18, 29,
      50-51, 64, 113
    self, 137-138
    self-actualization, 56
    self-confidence, 31, 51-52,
      56, 170
    social security benefits,
      61
    tastes, 26

185